PRAISE FOR ALI WENTWORTH

"Irresistible. . . . She is sharply observant and incisively funny. . . . Readers who like Nora Ephron and Laurie Notaro won't want to miss Wentworth."

—LIBRARY JOURNAL

"Wentworth spins hilarious tales of parenting, relationships, and, yes, getting older."

—PEOPLE

"Everything that comes out of Ali Wentworth's mouth is funny!"

—JERRY SEINFELD

"Razor-sharp."

—COSMOPOLITAN

GO ASK ALI

ALSO BY ALI WENTWORTH

HAPPILY ALI AFTER

ALI IN WONDERLAND

THE WASP COOKBOOK

HARPER

NEW YORK • LONDON • TORONTO • SYDNEY

GO ASK ALI

HALF-BAKED ADVICE
(AND FREE LEMONADE)

ALI WENTWORTH

HARPER

DISCLAIMER

Some of these stories are fact and some peppered with fiction. If you buy me a Magnolia Bakery icebox cake—I will tell you which is which.

To my daughters, Elliott and Harper
Who were born wiser than me . . .

CONTENTS

PART III: HALF-BAKED ADVICE

GO ASK ALI

IT'S NEVER TOO LATE FOR A HAPPY CHILDHOOD

I am not a truthsayer, therapist, or advice columnist. I'm not even particularly sage. But I do know a thing or two about a thing or two. And I have lived those things or two (or three) and consequently fallen on my face, been hurt, been humiliated, and occasionally been enlightened.

And for whatever reason, people tend to come to me for advice. (Probably because I act like I know more than I do or am married to a Rhodes Scholar.) Sometimes it's helpful; often it falls on deaf ears. The most frequent response is "Stop, you're so annoying." (Even my kids sometimes say this.) But because I'm cheaper than a shrink and make the best chocolate chip cookie dough in the Western Hemisphere, they tend to come back for more. Sure, everybody has their own official guide to living an ethical life. You can abide by the Ten Commandments, the Torah, the Koran, Deepak Chopra, whatever works for you. But nowhere in those aforementioned doctrines will they advise you on whether or not to teach your teenage daughter how to put in a tampon. Believe me, I've checked them all.

I have always found shared personal experience to be a valuable learning tool. And a very effective way to navigate life. I learn more about parenting and marriage from my girlfriends than from Google, my gynecologist, or Pope Francis. I know that Jesus suffered and there are tales to tell about that, but I like a more firsthand approach. And how to deal with extramarital affairs—well, the Dalai Lama won't return my texts. But I have women friends with real experience who can share some pretty daunting cautionary tales. And I have a few doozies based on my own exposure to life that I like to pass along.

Now, don't get me wrong here, I'm not trying to start a cult or replace Megyn Kelly on daytime TV, I just think that there is a much bigger impact when someone you know shares his or her experience. No doubt that's why the mom circles are so strong—it's the shared information. We do become a village raising our kids. It also humanizes us to be able to express our own fears, anxieties, and ignorance.

Think about the volcanic reaction to recent allegations of sexual predators. Of which, clearly, there are many and in every industry and faction of the workforce. A person speaks out and reveals a personal story and then, in a domino effect, more people speak out and it brings to light an epidemic.

Let me put the brakes on here for a second so that your expectations aren't too high about what you're about to read. Or listen to. Or just put on the shelf because the jacket is pretty and you need something to put under the photo of your cat. This is basically a humor book and sexual predators are only in the introduction to make a point. There is nothing religious, political, or ideological in the following pages. There might be one Republican joke, I can't remember.

Instead, I'm offering you the sum total of what I've figured out over the years. Things I know for sure, things I've learned the hard way, and the answers to questions others have posed to me over the years (yes, that's the half-baked advice part, but as I mentioned before, I am known for my baking skills . . .). Call it my sense and sensibility . . . or the mixed-up life of Ali Wentworth. But if you don't find at least one revelatory nugget, then I promise, I will come to your house and do your laundry. Within the tristate radius. Schedule permitting. And not including Jewish holidays. If I can't make it, I'll send my husband.

And if I can give you one piece of advice? You should buy this book for everyone you know. Or have ever met.

PART I

THIS MUCH I KNOW

PERSONALLY, I THINK THAT IF A WOMAN HASN'T MET THE RIGHT MAN BY THE TIME SHE'S TWENTY-FOUR, SHE MAY BE LUCKY!

—DEBORAH KERR

CHAPTER 1

GUTTING TO THE CHAPEL

When I arrived at Liz's apartment, her fiancé, Danny, told me she had been locked in the bathroom for more than two hours. I assumed she had a blemish she was gouging with tweezers and a bottle of witch hazel or was shaving her entire body. She is Armenian and hair is her nemesis.

"She's been crying and totally freaking out," he said, sounding somewhat concerned.

"I'm sure it's just nerves or a hygiene issue." I gently knocked on the bathroom door.

"Hey, Liz! I'm here! Herpes flare-up? Listen, the limo is

downstairs. Do you want me to take anything down? Do you have your veil on?"

The only noise from the bathroom was a running faucet and a few thumps. I believe the first thump was a white satin Jimmy Choo pump being thrown against the shower wall. The second might have been her head.

I waited downstairs in the black Cadillac limousine for what seemed like hours. Just me, the driver with no personality who smelled like pepperoni, and a blasting air conditioner that had my legs looking like something you'd find at a morgue. At last the car door opened and a large, disgruntled lace pastry shoved herself in. The driver started the ignition and we began our journey up Third Avenue.

"What the hell am I doing!" Liz wailed.

"You're getting married. You're just nervous."

Well, I knew it wasn't nerves. This was the state of a woman en route to a hanging, not her wedding. Not dead man walking, but rather dead woman being driven in a fancy car.

"I don't want to do this, I don't . . . I don't . . . I don't want to do this!"

"Liz, listen, do you want me to get you a pill? Do you have your Lexapro with you? Or Xanax? What about those pills you take when you fly?"

"I'm making a big mistake," she shrieked as she grabbed the handle of the car door.

"Whoa, whoa, whoa . . . don't try to open that. That's a

really expensive dress and you're going to get blood all over it. Now take a deep breath."

Liz took a deep breath and stared out the car window, anxious and distraught, the way I assumed O. J. Simpson felt in the white Bronco.

"You don't have to do this," I whispered.

"Yes, I do," she whimpered back. "There are three hundred people coming."

"That's not a reason to get married."

"It's costing my dad sixty dollars a plate!"

"Well, that is definitely the best reason to get married."

We drove the rest of the way up Madison Avenue in silence. Occasionally Liz would blow her nose or reapply lip gloss. After hours of weeping her face was a piece of modern art, a Franz Kline with mascara smeared across one side of her cheek, eyeliner dripping down toward her ears. I thought to myself, If I ever feel even one percent of the agony she's feeling, I have to promise myself not to go through with the marriage. And I will open the car door and roll onto the highway going sixty miles an hour if need be. But then I won't get any wedding cake. So I'd grab the cake, eat the top two tiers and perhaps a bread basket, then hurl myself out of the moving limo.

Years later, the expedition to my own wedding could not have been more different. I was not just serene, I was determined. I was chomping at the bit to marry this man I had instantaneously fallen in love with. And as the car made its way through the streets of Manhattan to the Greek Orthodox cathedral where I was to be legally and spiritually bound, I remembered my journey all those years before with Liz. It had been so torturous. A few years earlier when I had recognized similar feelings of trepidation during an engagement, I had had the wherewithal to end it. Thanks to a gutsy gut. Not an easy feat, but in the end, everyone benefited. We are all married with children and enviable Instagrams now.

In the meantime, Liz got divorced. Not a shock to anyone. Except to Danny. But a stable of Russian hookers and a steady supply of Ecstasy no doubt got him through it.

I recently reconnected with an old acting-school friend. She and I had participated in the same thespian summer program, an institution that pirated my parents' money and taught me nothing. Well, that's not entirely true—I learned all the words to *Jesus Christ Superstar*. I spent sweltering afternoons pacing around a crappy "loft" space in midtown Manhattan pretending to be a tiger or a brush. And squeaking through the lyrics of *Les Miserables*. Not one of the Stanislaski tools that was hammered into my head have I used. Ever. My years of drama school could have been condensed into one word: pretend. Oh, okay, I get it! I'll just pretend. Done.

I ran into Kirby in the gift shop of the Metropolitan

Museum of Art. I could lie and say I was there to peruse the sixteenth-century armor of Emperor Ferdinand
the first, but I just wanted to use the bathroom. She was
mulling over a postcard of lilacs in a window by Mary
Cassatt—turning it over and over again, studying it from
every possible angle. You would have thought she was considering buying the actual painting. Kirby was still shockingly thin and meticulously put together—a chic blend of
navy and black with a hint of bohemia in the form of a
Mexican straw handbag. We sat in the Met café and over
the next hour caught up on twenty years. She sipped black
coffee with some diet sweetener that was made from bugs
or worms or something and I drank my Earl Grey tea with
heaps of sugar and cream.

I feigned interest in her mind-blowing year in Rome
(yes, we all learn so much about ourselves when sleeping
with the married literature professor mostly because he
owned a Vespa) and her parents' health problems. And I
struggled through the endless description of her rigorous
physical regimen and Mediterranean diet that explains why
people still ask her to model. But it was the story about her
month-long marriage that jolted me awake. She had dated
a freakishly tall man for a couple of years. (I say freakishly
tall because she showed me a photo and his body was about
nine feet long, topped by a tiny mango of a head.) "When
he first took off his pants, did you think you'd see stilts?"
They liked each other; he proposed. I couldn't get past the

fact that she liked, sorry, "loved" him. I'm not superficial in that way, but it would be impossible to see past (or up, above, and around) it.

Prepping for the wedding, she told me, she'd been a zombie. She felt nothing—not joy, not excitement, just dread. It wasn't until she was walking down the aisle that she felt something: she burst into tears. Not tears of joy (something I've never actually witnessed), but pure terror. Kirby confessed that she knew she was embarking on a monumental mistake, but "the dress was bought, my parents flew across the country . . ." All the stellar reasons to bind oneself in wedlock for eternity.

Kirby had always been beautiful and I think that sometimes when you rely only on what's on the outside, the internal feeling of self-worth is anemic. She wore what was chic, she drank Northern Californian wine, she read the books everyone was reading and voted the way her liberal friends did even if she had no clue what Prop 8 entailed. So when a striking man (in the form of a professional basketball player or Beetlejuice) arrived on the scene during the appropriate age of marriage (Martha Stewart has put it somewhere between ages twenty-two and twenty-nine), she said, "I guess I do."

Sometimes the pangs are not so subtle. I had befriended a textile designer years ago during my "always a bridesmaid, never a bride" phase of life. Or as some would call it, my twenties. Lucy was very acerbic and brittle, with the palest skin I'd ever seen. There was almost a lavender sheen to it. When Lucy lay in the sun, nothing happened. She didn't tan, burn, or freckle, she just stayed the same alabaster color. Like a vampire or Ichabod Crane. Lucy was one of those brassy girls you're relieved to be friends with because she eviscerated her enemies. You know, keep your friends close, but your enemies closer until they just blend and you can't remember which was which?

Lucy decided to marry Willy. Willy was also slightly terrified of her. I think Willy had a complicated relationship with his mother. Lucy and Willy were constantly spatting, but I chalked it up to them being a "lively" couple. Although the scenario wasn't vicious fights followed by peel-the-paint-off-with-your-fingernails makeup sex. It was just vicious fights. Full stop. And they were eye rolling way too soon. You're not supposed to roll your eyes when your partner leaves the room until a good ten years in. They weren't even living together, let alone married, and they were like Archie and Edith Bunker. I was too young then to even consider that this was a doomed coupling. What did I know? My best functioning relationship with a man up to that point was with my older brother. A brother I lived with, sharing one pan, a toilet, and very thin walls. So, barely functioning.

The afternoon of their nuptials, I came early to help her with the finishing touches. And by finishing touches I mean I set up the whole wedding. The ceremony and dance party were being held in Lucy's postage-stamp-size back-yard. There were paper lanterns, homemade guacamole, Mexican Jesus candles—you know, everything you'd see on a budget DYI wedding on Pinterest.

I was arranging the place cards (white stones with names messily painted on them) when Lucy yanked me into her bathroom.

"Oh God!"

"What? You saw the cake?"

"No, no, no . . . Why? What's wrong with the cake?"

"Nothing. It's great. It's bright orange?"

"WHAT?!?"

"It's fine, it's just not exactly the pale pink you ordered. . . . What's the matter?"

"I couldn't sleep all night. I don't know what I'm doing. . . ."

"Lucy, this is normal. It's just wedding jitters."

"It's not. It's not jitters. I don't want to marry Willy."

"What do you mean? Why?"

"I made out with a woman last night. . . ."

My brain started to scramble. I had been prepping my answers for "I'm too young," "What if he falls out of love with me?," or "Are fajitas festive enough?" For this, I had nothing.

"Well, you . . ."

"I think I like women."

"Are you sure?"

Lucy smiled widely. "Oh yes, I'm sure!"

"Well, then you have to tell Willy!"

"But people are coming in three hours!"

Again, why does the fact that guests are coming seem to trump the moral dilemma of 'til death do us part?

I stood in the itsy-bitsy garden holding a bunch of daisies and my mouth shut. The sense of doom spoiled my appetite for the cheese taquitos. So I took them to go. Along with some cake. And the Mexican candles.

Spoiler alert: Three months later, Lucy and Willy divorced.

What, you may ask, is my point?

Don't underestimate the power of the gut. The visceral voice that perhaps doesn't speak your language but interprets your feelings on their most basic level. Fear, sadness, unhappiness, discontent . . . If these women had listened to their gut, they would have saved themselves some pain, some money, and twenty pounds of salmon mousse. It has taken me years to sort through the layers of mishegas (Mom, this is Yiddish for craziness) to be able to interpret the emotions that I rely on as warning signs. They were nonexistent when I was a teenager (see: that time I hitchhiked to Provincetown at midnight and shoplifted five cashmere sweaters at once). Blame it on the undeveloped frontal lobe.

So today if you invite me to your wedding and in a

panicked state confide that you don't want to go through with it? I'm telling you now, I will throw you in the trunk of my rental car, drive you through El Paso, Texas, and across the border, and dump you in the Chihuahuan desert. You will thank me.

Assuming you make it back.

CHAPTER 2

INSTA-SLAM

People always joke about the effects of social media—
"Oh my God, I'm addicted to Instagram"—well, guess
what, you are. Every time you swipe, you're getting the
same adrenaline rush as when you play the slot machines.
Or stumble across Oreos dipped in dark chocolate at the
grocery store. Listen, I hate Instagram. I have yet to find
one redeeming thing about it. I thought maybe it would
offer a simple way for my parents to keep up with the tri-
umphs of their flourishing grandchildren. You know, give
them bragging rights and screen savers. But it only opened
the door to endless scrutiny: "That ocean is freezing, are
you sure they should be swimming this time of year?"
"The girls look very thin, are they eating?"

My fourteen-year-old daughter forced an account upon me a few months ago, which is the source of endless frustration because I don't even know my own password and I keep accidentally posting things twice. Okay, I confess: I was so intrigued by my friends' posts of blooming gardens, homemade apricot chicken dishes, and selfies in front of the Caribbean sunset that I was happy to sign on. There was a voyeuristic quality I found enticing. You gotta keep up with the Joneses (and their friends and their friends and their friends). And soon I was following people I've never met! I didn't even know what city they lived in or their full names, but I knew they got a new puppy, liked competitive bike riding, and were overly invested (to a disturbing degree) in their Halloween costumes. My daughter signed me up to follow some Victoria's Secret models (new icons to our youth), which does wonders for any middle-aged woman's ego. Nothing like walking the dogs in baggy sweatpants and a retinol face mask while you scroll through images of bikini-clad models doing yoga. Why am I wasting my time, time that could be used to clean out my kids' closets or get those cavities filled, on the idealization of COMPLETE STRANGERS!?! Because it's addictive? If more than five hundred million photos are being uploaded every day, we all (as a culture) obviously need to communicate this way. Yet how disturbing it is that we allow our emotional well-being to be determined by how many followers we get. That is a dangerous, slippery slope. (By the way, if you're reading this, please follow me @TheRealAliWentworth. My whole worth depends on it.)

The performed lives we see on Instagram are heavily curated. And not true. It's an opportunity to play "Whose life is better?" and the stakes are high because this game can lead to isolation and despondency. What are we all trying to prove? We know it's a farce; they know they're posting a form of fiction. . . . When was the last time you saw a post of someone in the throes of food poisoning or crying on the toilet? Or any sliver of authentic life? It's like being blasted with everyone's Christmas card fifty times a day.

Before long, everything becomes an opportunity for a brilliant Insta and it doesn't even matter if you have acne, blemishes, or just don't like your freckles—there's a filter for everything! There are apps like SkinneePix, which will shave off fifteen pounds, and DXP, which will make you look dreamy. With all the warm filters and aesthetic manipulation at your literal fingertips, you can just photoshop your life!

I posted (approved) pictures of my daughters surfing and laughing uproariously while we all shucked corn last summer. Each post was meticulously chosen to present the Merchant-Ivory version of our life. (My girls would call it the Kardashian version.) Even my lawn looked lusher and greener, courtesy of the Perpetua filter. I didn't post my fourteen-year-old daughter having a complete meltdown when I interrogated her on the whereabouts of her summer-reading book report, or the face her sister wore while she gave me the silent treatment for canceling a sleepover. Nor did I zoom in close enough to betray the fact that my lush lawn was sprinkled with dog shit. My life presented like the cover of *Southern Living* magazine. And I live way up north.

I have a routine to the start of each day. First I awake in a panic—was there a terrorist attack, did I take my pill last night, did I remember to buy maple syrup? My ritual also includes spending as much time in my pajamas as possible. My children are usually still asleep when my alarm goes off at 6:00 A.M. most days of the week, most months of the year. Year after year. I pitter-patter to the kitchen to fill my *GMA* mug with PG Tips and sugar and cream. No food to accompany it. Just tea. (Don't worry, a huge amount of carbs comes later.) And then I start with emails. Sometimes followed by a quick swipe through Instagram. Then news. Okay, I do a drive-by on Dailymail.uk.com.

One morning, however, I settled into a rattan chair on the porch and fell straight down the Insta hole. Perhaps because it was summer and the posts were particularly luminous, sprinkled with exotic travel shots. I had a plethora of people I followed: my besties, interior designers whose style I covet, and a few celebrities (just to remind me how mundane and monotonous my own life was). At warp speed I robotically hit the little heart symbol on every photo I passed. And then I stopped at a snapshot of a party.

I recognized everyone in the pic. I was head scratching over the name of one particular man, then tapped on the screen and got full recognition. (Instagram actually names names.) Why was he there; the hostess doesn't even like him? Everyone was beaming, holding wineglasses, arms draped across one another's shoulders. I felt that pang in my stomach. Why wasn't I in the photo? Where was I? SAD EMOJI, SAD EMOJI, SAD EMOJI! I hadn't felt that gutted since I was in middle school and spotted Lucy's birthday invite (which I never received) smack in the center of Sadie's ladybug-themed bulletin board. Perhaps I had underestimated my place in the world.

I'm not a person who likes to dwell on unhappy feelings. Someone once told me that if you let a negative thought fester in your mind, it will eventually turn into brain cancer. And I don't want brain cancer.

So I called the hostess of the affair that, in my mind, had become the greatest dinner party (next to Capote's black and white ball) to ever take place.

"Of course you were invited!" she swore. "You were in Los Angeles, remember? I just didn't post it for a couple of weeks." Complete embarrassment. Did I need to up my meds? Why did I allow the post to rattle my cage so badly? Yes, they served chicken curry and the kinds of cheese that I would commit murder for, but the real point was being tagged in a faux joyous moment. Or as the kids might say, a wicked case of FOMO.

A few weeks ago I experienced a perfect Instagram storm. I had found an old photo from the 1950s of four women with teased-out-high hairdos and go-go boots that was hysterical. I tagged four friends I thought resembled the crazy gals in the photo. I was expecting the usual #LMAO. Instead I got a text from another close friend who was crushed that she was not part of the silliness, not one of the women "tagged." At first I was taken aback. We are grown-ups! Didn't we work through this in middle school? I immediately sent her a text of love and heart emojis and an explanation. And as I was waiting for a text back, I started to scroll through the feed of "My perfect life" posts when I stopped at a photo of one of my BFFs on a rowboat in Central Park with her husband and kids and various godparents. I remembered it had been one of her teenage daughters' birthdays. They were cuddled up in thick turtleneck sweaters holding wineglasses (not the teenagers) and laughing, laughing, laughing. And in the far corner of the snapshot I could barely make out the face of a woman my friend had met recently at work and instantly become enamored with. What the hell was she doing there? It was just family? And if they were going to open the red velvet rope it would be for close friends, not freshly new, unbaked acquaintances! So while I was waiting to hear from the girlfriend I had triggered with my tagged photo, I texted my friend whose photo had triggered me. And just before I hit the send button I started laughing out loud, alone like the insane woman I know I'm going to be in thirty years. I screamed, "I hate Instagram!" And threw the phone under one of my pillows. And then I heard the faint sound of a *ping* (which means someone just posted something) and I dove onto the bed digging for the phone like a pig for a white truffle.

I am so grateful that social media wasn't as omnipresent when I was single as it is now. If I had to scroll through the ex-boyfriend and his new girlfriends? It would give them real faces and ruin the images of the hideous trolls that I held so dear and that kept me from living in my bathtub with an endless supply of Cheetos. It's too much! Not only do the hills have eyes, but the sky, grass, and sun do, too, and they're all going viral!

———

My daughters begged us for Instagram accounts. The argument being that all their friends had them. This seemed a valid enough reason for my husband and me, who capitulate (much like our Senate does now) to them daily. We agreed, with the one caveat that the accounts had to be private. Of course, private these days means public to anyone who knows anyone who knows you. But we draw the line at that third degree of separation.

One night at dinner we were discussing the story of the group of boys who were admitted to Harvard and then un-admitted when the university saw racist and offensive comments posted on their social media.

My eldest daughter cocked her head. "How did Harvard even know they were posting these things?"

"Honey, colleges look into all your social media when you apply! They are not going to accept someone with pornographic images or offensive remarks."

She looked spooked. "They look at all that stuff?"

"Of course!"

Later that evening she came into my room, her eyeballs particularly large.

"Umm . . . can colleges find stuff that you deleted?"

She had not let this conversation die and clearly she had a dog in the hunt. But she's an innocent fourteen-year-old, so I couldn't fathom what she could have posted that she was sweating over.

"What's going on? Did you put something on social media that I need to be concerned about?"

She looked down sheepishly. "I think so."

"Oh my God, what? How many times have I told you about the dangers of putting images out into the ether? Those photos live forever! What did you do?"

"Well, I have a mole on my butt and I can't see it with a mirror, so I took a photo of it with my phone because I wasn't sure if it was a mole or a pimple. But I deleted it right away!"

I smiled. "You're fine. But if you want to start investigating your vagina, use a mirror."

She got it. And I stopped imagining her getting un-admitted to Stanford because she was checking for melanoma.

I check their feeds every day, it seems. My youngest makes ugly faces and showcases cupcakes, alongside her obsession with tiny Japanese puppies and slime. Observing her liking of thousands of Instagrams in rapid succession one weekend morning, I was reminded of those manic old men in Vegas who have been at the blackjack table all night . . . "Hit me . . . Hit me . . . Hit me . . ." She was in Insta rehab last summer at camp, where she was separated from devices for seven weeks and had to do things like breathe air and look her friends in the eye. She sweated and had the shakes but pronounced herself clean the fourth week in.

Instagram is today's "I'll have what she's having." Except you can't because what she's having has been doctored. As long as we all understand that, then bring on the filters! But don't freak out when one of your followers comments, "Wow! You look so different in person!" (Translation: In real life.) So proceed with caution. My generation are the guinea pigs of social media. We didn't grow up with it (thank God), and so the ramifications are based on our experiences. Like Gillette razors on bunnies. And like most pharmaceutical commercials these days: Instagram side effects may include: headaches, diarrhea, low self-esteem, isolation, jealousy, shingles, loss of sexual appetite, insomnia, nausea, blue screen coma, and suicidal thoughts. Take in at small doses. Warning—highly addictive.

CHAPTER 3

KINDNESS

I don't believe in karma, mercury in retrograde, or the healing powers of hemp, but one thing I do believe in is kindness. I know, it sounds trite, a sentiment that should be relegated to mugs and refrigerator magnets, but trust me, stick with it and you can't go wrong. I'm not saying you should become a missionary or donate all your organs— I'm not talking extreme-sports kindness. Acts of kindness won't guarantee that your life will be perpetually blessed. But they will make it eleven percent better.

I live in New York City, where kindness is as rare as grass. People scream profanities if you so much as glance at their latte at Starbucks, strangers give each other the finger the way casual neighbors wave at a small-town parade on

Veterans Day. In other words, speak softly and carry a big motherfucking stick! So accessing kindness can be a Herculean task. And I don't mean dropping change in a homeless person's cup or picking up your dog's poop even when nobody is watching. Those are conscience soothers, not acts of authentic, active kindness. That requires turning it up a notch. When someone in line at the grocery store is a nickel short, give it to her. If someone is struggling to cross the street, help him. If you see anybody potentially in harm's way, scream, jump, call the police. Never capitulate to the notion of "Well, that ain't my business."

Resources vary, of course, especially when it comes to actual giving. I believe generosity is a tributary of kindness. I admire people who donate anonymously—billionaires who don't need the roar of applause or a building named after them—just as much as I admire someone who donates his or her time to a local women's shelter.

And sure, it's easy to lose it when the waitress gives you Russian dressing instead of blue cheese. But really, what's the point? Why should the fallback reaction be hostility? As Jackie DeShannon memorably wrote, "Put a little love in your heart and the world will be a better place." But that was the sixties. That way of thinking only works now if you're stoned or live in Canada.

Kindness in acts. Kindness in words. Kindness in how you live in the world. Give it a try. As always, however, there are exceptions. You can be severely unkind to anyone who talks during a movie, chews too loudly, or wears sandals on an airplane. In these cases, go ahead and throw shade.

Sometimes an act of kindness can backfire. But that should never deter you. I am living proof.

Back in 2008, I was living in Washington, D.C., with my husband and our firstborn, then a pudgy Buddha, and pregnant with another. For the entirety of George W. Bush's presidency, the city had been reserved and restrained, as if living under house arrest. I think we were the only people having sex in the whole city. But Barack Obama had just been elected the forty-fourth president of the United States and there was a palpable new energy to the town.

I was fired up and hormonally unbalanced. It was a few days after the inauguration and I had heard from insiders that the Obamas didn't know many people in D.C. except for the Chicagoans they brought with them. I could relate; when I moved to Los Angeles years earlier, I only knew my brother, and we shared a bungalow in a sketchy part of Hollywood. True, I wasn't president, but everyone can relate to being the new kid in town. Even one who sits in the Oval Office and holds the nuclear codes.

I was shopping in the posh section of D.C., Georgetown, where adorable boutiques alternate with the university's frat houses along the cobblestoned streets. I walked into a particularly preppy shop adorned with more Lilly

Pulitzer than a West Palm Beach AA meeting. And there it was hanging on the wall. A sleeveless blue and white cocktail dress cut like an Oscar de la Renta. The thought hit me like a thunderclap. I would buy that dress for the new First Lady as a welcome to our nation's capital gift! No, I wasn't drunk. No, I had no fever. No, it wasn't a pregnancy side effect. I pulled the dress off the hanger and held it up. I knew the First Lady had famously svelte and muscular arms, so sleeveless wouldn't be a problem. I surmised that she was about a size 6. I watched with joy as the retailer, in a fuchsia headband adorned with a large gold toad (not sure how she kept her head up), wrapped the dress up like it was a baby on baptism day, white silk ribbon and all. If she only knew the ingenious plan I had hatched right next to her display of monogrammed water bottles in the shape of lobsters.

Now, for obvious reasons, you can't send just anything to the White House, but luckily I had an acquaintance who worked in the social office of the new administration. I asked him to present my festive package to Michelle Obama like frankincense for the baby Jesus.

I was so excited. Like the day after my first date with my husband when he had mentioned Krispy Kreme doughnuts and I had two dozen sent to his office. Not that the box of doughnuts sealed the deal, but the fact that I had listened and taken note and had the whimsy to send them made up for my rather small breasts.

Now, before you label me a fool, let me remind you that this was a situation wherein my intent was purely selfless. I might seem like the nosey parker who brings a Bundt cake to her new next-door neighbor in order to sniff around for gossip to spew at the next block party, but I had no agenda. I neither expected nor wanted anything. Dammit, what woman wouldn't want to receive the gift of a new dress? For goodness sake, worst case, it still had tags! It was returnable for store credit!

It took a few days for the dress to pass inspection with the security detail. Or so I imagined—I never actually heard anything. They probably have it locked away in a bombproof box at the FBI. Fine. I was naive. But I stand behind my intentions. In spite of the fact that for years that dress has been a source of constant fodder and ridicule among my friends. To this day whenever Michelle Obama is on TV one of them texts me, "Is she wearing THE dress?" But would I change the sequence of events if I could? Absolutely not.

Years ago I was told a story that had a profound impact on my worldview. The story involved a man who, destitute and brought low in life, was committed to a psychiatric facility. He had lost his job and his family, and was crippled by depression. In the hospital he befriended another patient, an artist, and they became close. After a year, the artist was discharged, leaving the man alone once again. But before he left, the artist handed the man a canvas he had painted during his stay. A colorful and abstract painting. The man cherished it.

A year later the man was also discharged, wary of what bad luck awaited him beyond the wrought-iron-barred windows. After a series of wrong turns, he was forced to sell the painting to get back on his feet. But the sale of the painting enabled the man to start his own business, buy a house, and, eventually, start a new family. He was blessed with a chance of a new life.

The artist's name was Willem de Kooning. In fact, the story could have ended with the mere act of the artist giving the man the painting. In this case, the painting ended up being worth hundreds of thousands of dollars. But you never know what an act of kindness will lead to—maybe not a painting that now hangs in the Museum of Modern Art—but perhaps a fleeting momentary feeling of well-being.

Now, I am in no way comparing myself to de Kooning. It's just a lovely, selfless story that stands on its own. And I think it encapsulates the kindness that's becoming so tenuous these days. You should still be wary when a stranger offers you candy (unless they're Milk Duds and in that case it's worth the risk). But there is something to the notion of practicing random acts of kindness, otherwise it would not be written somewhere in every yoga studio in the country.

CHAPTER 4

MAINE

Every summer we spend a weekend in Maine with my mother and stepfather. The predictability of these annual visits is an unfailing source of comfort. That, and we shove as many lobsters and steamers into our mouths as humanly possible.

My mother and stepfather have been going to Maine in the summer for the past twenty years. It used to be Cape Cod, but Maine is slower, more temperate, and not as crowded with the hordes of college students elbowing one another for jobs scooping ice cream and throwing frozen clams into huge vats of oil.

The best thing about our visits is that my children are afforded very little luxury and absolutely no WiFi service.

They pad around in bare feet and are "encouraged" by their grandmother to pick blueberries, clear the table, and help out around the house. And they are at their most polite. You will never witness either of my daughters giving their grandmother, Muffie, any sass. Even when my mother is careening around the dirt roads of Tenants Harbor popping deviled eggs into her mouth as she drives with one hand at about seventy miles an hour, my children are polite and quiet. This could be because they are contemplating their mortality. But I like to think they are simply gracious children.

On our last trip my mother insisted on taking my kids to the local dump. A place I remember all too well—though the one I frequented weekly as a child was in Plymouth, Massachusetts. We would grab the foul-smelling garbage bags and hurl them onto a heap of trash heavily guarded by seagulls. You saw everything from old lobster shells to mattresses to (once) a dented rowboat. Although steeped in a retching stench, the dump was an endless source of wonderment.

The one in Maine did not disappoint. Not only was there the obligatory mountain of rusty mufflers, decaying shopping carts, and broken lobster traps, but they had a store next door that sold the salvageable trinkets. There were huge posters for movies and jazz festivals in moldy frames behind smashed glass, rusted Christmas cookie tins, and baskets that used to hold floral arrangements from the town florist. My mother excitedly scooped up an old ice bucket she was eyeing for compost. She got it for fifty cents. My daughters picked their way through the narrow shelves gingerly, so as not to risk smearing schmutz on their leggings.

My children never knew my mother when she was fancy. When she wore gowns, danced with royalty, and walked through the White House Rose Garden with various presidents. To them, Grandma always wears jeans, brags about her sweater score from the Goodwill, and serves food from the fridge that expired months ago. And I love that they know this version of my mother. Sure, she still has the trappings of a well-heeled upbringing, a higher education, and the worldliness of an avid traveler, but she has retained all the important things in life and released all the frivolity. She is someone who doesn't fuss over coffee-mug rings on a Winslow table that should be in the Boston Museum of Fine Art.

But the greatest gift she awards my children is a sense of their heritage, the stories of the relatives who lived before them. No visit is complete without a full-blown oral history presentation, augmented by an arcade of photographs, cockeyed and warped paintings, a chipped teapot, and a captain's bed, all bursting with stories and mythology.

And she makes them aware of the history beyond their own. As we barrel down the back roads, she points to colonial houses with chipped white paint and worm-eaten barns. "That's where George Washington slept in 1789," she'll say, pointing toward a hilltop mansion while swerving wildly to avoid hitting a seafood truck straight-on. We'll stop at the side of a road joint that sells bait, tackle, and ice cream. The freezer burn makes the ice cream sandwiches look jaundiced, but as my daughters prune their faces she laughs. "Oh, come on, they are perfectly fine! Ice cream is ice cream."

I will never forget one visit when my mother wanted to surprise the girls with homemade pancakes. She used an unbuttered nonstick frying pan and the pancakes were burned black on the outside and dripping raw on the inside. If these were made at home, the girls' plates would have been hastily pushed away, followed by endless complaining and a mass exodus to their rooms. In Maine they ate every forkful. And no amount of maple syrup could cover the taste of charcoaled Bisquick. But they knew that making their grandmother feel confident and appreciated would outlast the pasty metallic taste.

My mother and stepfather have a small schooner that they take out less frequently now that age has assaulted their muscles and chipped away at their sense of balance. But we went out this summer. The girls curled up under towels in the bow as we sailed along the quintessential rocky coast, passing majestic lighthouses and elfin islands crowded with so many pine trees that they looked like birthday cakes for centenarians. Every once in a while my mother would shriek and point to the slick head of a baby seal bobbing in the waves or a bald eagle soaring over our heads. And my children would search for the animals, their mouths open and eyes wide. We anchored by a little island that actually had a beach—well, a pebbled beach. And laughed hysterically as their father (my Rhodes Scholar husband) struggled against the tide to row us to shore. Political commentators are his friends, not oars.

We walked the surf line of the beach finding green sea urchins that had been discarded by seagulls. The ones still round and intact were true treasures. We collected them in a plastic bag, which I eventually placed in Tupperware, carefully wrapped in tissue paper as if they were living organs being transported to the nearest hospital. My younger daughter lay on a large, smooth boulder with her bare feet in the air singing to herself what sounded like a camp song she had learned earlier in the summer. My eldest nibbled on chocolate chip cookies while she listened to my mother talk about clamming and how Maine was losing its hold on the lobster market.

"Because of global warming, the lobsters are heading out farther and farther into the sea and the lobstermen then have to go out farther and farther to get them, which costs them money and time. It's such a shame. You guys need to help the planet and stop global warming." My daughter nodded; wondering how she would possibly be able to help these lobstermen when she became the editor in chief of *Vogue*.

We slowly made our way back to the harbor. Camden Harbor is part of what is known as Maine's Gold Coast; it has high-end shops filled with duck decals, hand-embroidered throws, polished sea glass, and the kind of bookstore you can spend a full day in. And for some unknown reason, the triple scoops of Moose Tracks ice cream just taste better in Maine.

"Maybe we can go shopping," my older daughter (who is our resident fashionista) blurted out as we secured the ropes to the dock.

"Oh, you don't want to buy anything in town, you can make it all yourself." And that was that. My mother can take you to the most remote, unheralded antiques store, the one so off the beaten path that you have to call first to have them unlock the barn, but she has little interest in the commercial stuff.

Two of my best friends, Katie and Michelle, hail from a small island in Maine. I instantly fell in love with them as we all made our way in the shark-infested waters called Hollywood. They were taking the more noble path of nonprofit and philanthropic endeavors, I was dressing in thrift-shop dresses with crazy cat-lady glasses auditioning to be a receptionist on shows like *Dharma & Greg*. We would spend hours around a small farmhouse table in Santa Monica talking love, heartache, and sometimes even politics. If the politics related somehow to the heartache or the love. I have witnessed them flourish in their careers, marry, and have children and all the joy and upheaval that comes with it. There is something resolute and puritan about them that is so familiar. They are, as they say, solid people—and I'm proud to live on the same planet as them. They are my rocks. And they come from rocks. Literally. They are "pull yourself up by your bootstraps" and "get this shit done" kind of gals.

The morning we were at the dump I assumed they were still at the billionaire think tank convention in the Midwest, where they share ideas with great minds like Bill Gates and Malala Yousafzai. But, funnily enough, Michelle texted me from the dump in Mount Desert Isle, Maine, where she has built herself a home overlooking the water and hidden by sprawling pines. She is in her element at the local hardware store, which she finds "wicked cool." So Michelle and my mother, women I regard with such admiration and esteem, were both simultaneously chucking their crap into a big hole in the ground. Kind of a metaphor for life.

These are the women who have taught me the integral

components of a full life: history, the earth, legacy, truth, and love. And when the materialism, WiFi, and other trappings of my children's generation are stripped away from them, they do the most remarkable things. They experience pleasure on its most fundamental level. Like helping a moth find safe passage from the garage to the freedom of the outdoors. And experiencing the joy in picking blueberries off the bush and putting them into their mouths until their lips turn blue. To appreciate a smooth gray rock, encircled with white lines, which used to be a talisman for sailors who clutched them for good luck as they left their families to sail out to sea.

In this world my children have access to their roots, their dreams, and their creative ideas. Imagine a world where lavender barnacles are more fascinating than who slapped who on *The Real Housewives of Beverly Hills*.

We had discarded all the stinky garbage from our lobster feast the night before. My mother honked the horn and we strolled out of the dump's thrift shop. My younger daughter tugged on my hand.

"Mom, I saw this little blue chipped lamp in there that would look nice in my room, can I borrow a dollar?"

And the beat goes on.

Families are complex. Thanksgiving is always a letdown, I don't care how amazing your pumpkin pie is. But it's important to know your roots, your history, where you hail from. It informs the person you become. Unless you're a Dahmer, in which case you should keep it to yourself. For better or worse, I know who I am in part by the stories and myths handed down from generation to generation. Note to my daughters: The captain of the Mayflower—William Bradford—is our direct descendent, so cool it with the "the pilgrims were cannibals"! It's upsetting Grandma.

CHAPTER 5

MONA

At some point—make that at multiple points—in your life you've been asked, Who's your hero? Your mentor? Your inspiration? And how many times did you have to respond diplomatically with the perfunctory answer Helen Keller or Harriet Tubman? And don't ask me which teacher's support allowed me to break the glass ceiling. I ended up breaking many glass objects, but only those within arm's reach. At my all-girls' boarding school the ceiling was stucco with fluorescent lighting, and none of the subpar teachers so much as loaned me a ladder to reach it. There was an art teacher who taught me how to blend charcoal shadowing, but then she ran off with one of my fellow classmates to live in a lesbian co-op in Amherst, Massachusetts. The rest of the teachers were more of the "no you can't" than the "yes you can!" variety. But I've never listened to the word "no." Unfortunately, or fortunately, my teenage daughters seem to have inherited that trait.

Nonetheless, heading into adulthood, people pressed me for archetypes. And by people, I mean college essays. I considered the usual suspects: Goldie Hawn, Lucille Ball, Imelda Marcos . . . but it always seemed contrived, conjuring up a role model responsible for the schizophrenic path I had taken. If I was being completely honest, I guess I would have had to thank the unaccredited child therapists I frequented in my youth.

(An aside: I am always suspicious of people who cite Louis Pasteur or Copernicus as their personal heroes. Really? Your "personal" heroes? You have a kinship with a Reformation-era mathematician and astronomer? Sure, they have impressive Wikipedia pages, but I doubt anybody has a real affinity with the heliocentric solar system. And if I read a college application where the student equated himself with Jean-Paul Sartre, I'd never stop throwing up.)

But then, in my forties, I met Mona.

The scene was a cocktail party for some convoluted charity or book signing or something important because Salman Rushdie and Barbara Walters were there. It was the kind of affair that calls for a black dress, kitten heels, and a swipe of blush. Nothing too flashy; a look that prizes subtlety and intelligence over moxie. These were events convened to show off one's ability to digest the latest op-ed and *New Yorker* pieces, not one's potential sexual abilities. So naturally, I was at ease.

My husband always gets cornered by the front door and that's where he's held hostage for the evening. I have restless-leg social syndrome so I have to move around. I am mostly hunting for the best hors d'oeuvres or a cheese platter I might have missed. Party food is my jam. I can happily park myself all night on an ottoman with a mini–porcelain plate of tiny bites. My favorites: baby potatoes stuffed with sour cream and cheap caviar, anything that involves prosciutto, and huge chunks of creamy cheeses that smell like ripe feet. And an ice-cold ginger ale. Not Schweppes, but Canada Dry. Score me this combo and I will kick my kitten heels off and sing "Lady Marmalade" at the top of my lungs whilst twerking.

I had just tiptoed into a small library and struck gold—a dessert table (and not just any dessert table: three different kinds of pies, bite-size cheesecakes, and gargantuan straw-berries dripping with dark chocolate)—when I heard the most harmonious laugh. Not fake cocktail chortle; real, guttural howls of joy. There was Mona. Short in stature, but giant in personality. Mona was petite with cropped, almost pixie, buttery blond hair and high cheekbones that framed her infectious smile. She wore black leggings and a large, crisp, white men's dress shirt and black velvet flats (an outfit I could make my uniform for the rest of my life).

Mona was cracking up with some foreign dignitary! Who probably didn't even speak English. I introduced myself to her—after all, she was the hostess and I had just devoured most of her desserts.

"I just wanted to introduce myself and thank you for inviting us."

Mona gave me a strong and enveloping hug like I was her long-lost abducted daughter suddenly set free.

"Oh, I finally get to meet ALI!" she said as if Ali were as infamous as Cher or Charo! "We were just discussing the benefits of having a mirror on the ceiling above your bed. People think it's wildly distracting, I think it's an enhancer! I have one and as long as I'm not on top, I love it!" The three of us burst into giggles. Mona was accessible and benevolent; people told her their deepest secrets and fears. And she never judged. She could have found something sympathetic about the Manson family as she served them chicken matzo ball soup. Her first question would have been "Why Squeaky? Lynette Alice Fromme is such a beautiful name."

Mona genuinely enjoyed every person she met. As a child psychiatrist, she was a listener and compassionate. She would have found Donald Trump fascinating. (I didn't say exemplary, I said fascinating.) She would have taken him out for dim sum and convinced him that instead of building a wall between the United States and Mexico, he should build a water park! Or thrown a brunch where she sat Trump between Jorge Muñoz, a former illegal immigrant and the founder of An Angel in Queens, a nonprofit that has served seventy thousand day laborers a warm meal since 2004, and Bette Midler (just for fun; for a little Bette and Donald sparring).

Mona personified life. She was the "if life is yogurt it's up to you to add the granola and nuts" kind of gal. She made you want to break out in song. She was the biggest optimist. If she were ever captured and held in a prison camp, she would have the enemy and captors holding hands in a circle. She would make pasta. And they'd all play Scruples. Mona had this palpable energy; she embodied chutzpah. You've never had sea urchin? Well, Mona would take you to the best sea urchin place in the city and clap as you savored your first gritty bite. She was passionate about art, music, people, politics, desserts . . . there was no subject she didn't relish and no person she would ever shun. She was a saint who loved a good blow-job joke.

Mona used to teach me Yiddish. She would call me mishpucka and mashugana. I love the Yiddish language; the words sound exactly like what they mean. When you schvitz you can hear the mist of water dripping off the back of your neck. And whenever I hear a Yiddish word, I think of Mona and her joyous punim.

Mona was known for her parties. Great, big happy parties. Where she would hang thousands of kites on the ceiling or fill enormous bowls with gold Hanukkah candy. She once threw a birthday party for her boyfriend who had once lamented that as a child he never had a toy train. Mona had a six-foot train doing loops down the dining room table all during dinner. The food was delicious, the ambience festive, but it was always the warmth of the beloved hostess that set the tone. You always left her parties as elated as the balloons that floated over the banister.

Mona wasn't famous (except to those who knew her). She never won a Nobel Peace Prize (though she should have). She was a psychiatrist. She not only loved people, she *knew* people. It was part of what made her so intent on understanding the human condition. And why she was so curious in general. She could make our seven-year-old daughter truly feel seen and heard. And most children that age don't ask to go visit an adult. Unless there's an enormous amount of candy involved. But my kids genuinely loved Mona.

I have an acquaintance named Jane. I don't know her well—in fact, I still don't know her last name. But I'm always happy to see her when I run into her. She is a natural beauty with bee-stung lips, green eyes, and a smattering of freckles. In other words, she looks like the woman in most organic face-cream ads.

I was walking in downtown Manhattan looking for a subway station when I bumped into her. Jane was wearing a butter-yellow sundress and large white sunglasses and recognized me first. I might have walked right by her had she not screamed my name. We hugged and smiled and chatted about the springlike weather. And then Jane surprised me by asking if she could get my opinion on something. "Of course," I replied, assuming it would be a Japanese salad-dressing recipe or a hotel recommendation in Chicago. Questions fitting the degree of our connection.

Instead, Jane started sobbing. "I'm so sorry, I'm so sorry," she repeated over and over. I quickly realized that miso and sesame oil would not be the answer.

"I'm pregnant." She sniffled.

"Fantastic," I said. "Congratulations!"

"No, it's not . . ." Jane looked down at the sidewalk and wiped her tears. "There's something wrong with the fetus."

"Oh no, Jane . . ."

"I'm Catholic! But . . . my doctor says the baby probably won't make it to term."

"Oh my God, I'm so sorry."

"My doctor wants me to have a late-term abortion." Jane started crying again. "What should I do?"

Now, this is not the usual banter for two women who rarely see each other and when they do they discuss Soul-Cycle and the genius of Bed Bath & Beyond. I was both taken aback and honored. Did I just happen upon her while she was grappling with a moral dilemma? Were we simply swirling particles that had collided at that second in time? Or were we somehow meant to have this microcosmic run-in? I thought about Mona and how she made people feel heard. And loved. And I thought about what Mona would say. And then I tried to imagine myself as a rabbi. Rabbi Wentworth. Oy.

I hugged her again. "Jane, that is the most heart-wrenching thing I've ever heard. Listen, I can't tell you what to do. Nobody can. The answer is somewhere inside of you. It's your truth. (Thank you, Oprah.) Maybe you should go somewhere to be alone and meditate. Think about what the life of this baby would/could be. And what is fair for this being and for you and for your family. Just know that no matter what path your life takes from this second on, it is the right path for whatever reasons you decide and you will be loved no matter what."

She hugged me tightly. In that moment she needed those words. Soothing words. And I needed chocolate cake. A very large piece.

Jane disappeared into the sea of tourists and I didn't set eyes on her again for months. And when I did run into her in a CVS she told me how significant colliding with me on the street that day had been. Not so much for steering her toward her ultimate decision, but for offering love and understanding as an outsider when she needed it the most. As we parted ways that day, I bowed and said, "Go with God."

Jane turned around. "Sorry, what?"

I cleared my throat, "See you soon, I hope!" I had gotten a little ahead of myself with the whole rabbi, priest, guru thing.

I remember when Mona was first diagnosed. I had extra-large sweatshirts made for both our families that said FUCK CANCER. She had days and weeks when she couldn't face visitors, so I would drop off an orchid or a shell my kids had painted with the doorman. I wanted Mona to know that I thought about her every single day. And I also believed she would beat that horrid disease because people like Mona don't deserve to be taken away.

Mona loved desserts. And she ate them with abandon. That was one of my favorite things about her. She didn't push the blueberry cobbler around on her plate or not order the tiramisu because she was feeling bloated. She ordered every dessert on the menu. It was not gluttonous—in truth she would only take small bites from each of them—it was more her spirited "the hell with it, let's all enjoy some sugar!" attitude. When she was very sick, I used to bring her homemade cakes that my daughters and I would decorate with gummy fish, sprinkles, and frosting flowers. She couldn't have any sugar because of her intense anticancer diet, but she loved to surround herself with baked goods—just looking at them made her happy. Perhaps her funeral should have been in a Parisian bakery. Maybe mine will be.

Mona died a few years ago. To date, it's the only funeral where I really bawled. That morning I had a nonsensical fight with my husband, which, I found out later, happened to a few couples who went to the funeral that day. We must have needed to push away any love to fully grieve for a woman who embodied nothing but love. I remember thinking during the funeral, This is a woman to emulate! This is a woman to worship! Knowing Mona had made me a better person. I wish you had gotten a chance to meet her.

My eleven-year-old daughter returned from sleepaway camp a couple of weeks ago. An all-girls, predominantly Jewish, uniformed camp straight out of the 1950s. I had missed her horribly and cursed sleepaway camp all summer long. But my daughter spent the sort of summer you yearn for your kid to have—she got to lead Shabbot and took first prize in the challah baking contest.

We were doing our annual back-to-school shopping at Staples (with the rest of America) when my daughter dropped a box of pencils that flew like pickup sticks in every direction. She looked up with a smile on her face and yelled, "Oy vey! Seriously?" I quickly turned around and for a second I thought it was Mona. . . .

These days it's a particularly arduous task finding mentors, heroes, people to aspire to. But if you discover a person who makes you want to be better, do better, feel better . . . then let them be the paragon. No, I don't mean taping a photo of Molly Sims on the fridge so you'll stop stress eating cubed cheese. Incorporate what you emulate. Mona chose fun. And so do I.

CHAPTER 6

SHH, I LOVE MY HUSBAND

I am one of those women who likes to talk. About anything. Someday, riddled with dementia, I'll just talk to myself and wear a shower cap to the grocery store, but for now I like an audience. I also like a gathering because it encompasses two of my favorite things—culinary delights and conversation. And I'll indulge any subject! You want to hit foreign policy, I'll give you my opinion on whether the U.S. should conduct targeted air strikes on Iran's nuclear weapons; if you want to talk interior design, even better. I say yes to fabric walls! I can go from *Star* magazine to the

Economist, dealer's choice. Although with the *Economist*, there will be a fair amount of bullshitting on my part.

My favorite thing is a ladies' lunch. Not my mother's ladies' lunch, which is why I probably should not use the word "ladies." I don't wish to sit around dressed in tweed eating cucumbers on white bread and discussing storm patterns and how trendy Talbots has become. I prefer when a group of my girlfriends and I get together, more often than not at my house so that I can make Ina Garten's infamous chocolate cake and linguine with clams (which I don't trust at restaurants) and go deep. I don't do chitchat; I don't care where someone bought her suede boots or what day of the cleanse she's on; I want us to speak honestly about the realities of being women, mothers, and wives. I want to know if you wake up covered in sweat, can have an orgasm without equipment, or are convinced you have an undiagnosed infectious disease. If you're content with your life choices, regretful, terrified of your own mortality. Are you angered by the lack of women on corporate boards? Sure, a little "Who does your Botox?" or "Where do you buy those soft sheets?" can be sprinkled in at the beginning, but after that I want to debate deeply personal issues as if it's a heated day in Congress. Well, Congress twenty years ago.

I've never been shy about expressing my thoughts, much to the horror of my parents, who were constantly covering their ears with their hands and chanting "This too shall pass." I'll regale my kids' bus driver, Otto, with my story of having to snap a chicken's neck when I was a teenager living on a farm in Nowheresville, Spain, or say something naughty on a late-night talk show. Some of my most existential conversations have been conducted with a posse of strangers I see at the dog park every day.

Lord knows, there's a plethora of issues to choose from these days. Yet the most compelling topics tend to involve what's wrong, rather than what's right, with the world: the government, the planet, health care, the economy, aging, annoying people, sexism, and the fact that marshmallow Peeps are only sold around Easter. And I'm game to chew on any of them! The Peeps, I mean.

However, there's one area of conversation that induces panic. When I hear words like "marriage" and "spouse," I start to sweat. You see, I have a dirty little secret. A secret that thwarts me from diving into some of the more titillating conversational waters. A secret I wouldn't even dare to write in a journal lest someone read it one day.

(Deep breath) I . . . I . . . I'm happily married. I know, I know. Boring, right? I don't know what to do! It's just something, for the life of me, I can't seem to change! I love my husband and he loves me. The end. Yawn. Dammit! Whenever the conversation at one of these girly soirees turns to the state of marital affairs (pun intended), I feel a wave of anxiety course through me like a first sip of bourbon. And it's usually around this time that I take a potty break.

Here's a typical scenario. Delia confides that her affair is now circling the third year. She's been meeting up with her lover at his apartment, in hotels, and once, while her husband was away, in her apartment. She has such a disastrous marriage and such a tantalizing affair that she gets to do most of the talking when we're all sucking down spaghetti pomodoro. She practically owns the event! I can't even slip in some faux advice. I haven't so much as looked at another man in sixteen years. So I sit there in silence. What is wrong with me—I can't even muster up a crush on Idris Elba (Google him)! Or Megan Fox!

Lydia's husband left her with two small children. She's lost twenty pounds and (for reasons I don't understand) also her adult acne. We talk for hours about her ex-husband's new, much younger girlfriend and how much he'll regret choosing boobs over substance. How he is a despicable, un-Christian fool and she should have known that when she met him in college and he was the head of a fraternity. Lydia's situation is endlessly captivating and sympathetic; her ex-husband's girlfriend's Facebook affords us hours of speculation. We can devote an entire meal to a dissection of "that woman's" makeup blog, her forty followers, and the fact that her lips are so inflated they've taken up half her face.

And then every once in a while someone in the group will turn to me and inquire about my husband and my marriage. "Well," I answer sheepishly. I riffle through my list of grievances—he won't do dishes, sometimes he uses my toothbrush—but these sound so amateur next to Lydia's husband blindsiding her for a much younger woman he's been dating for almost as long as they were married. It renders me silent. A state I find most uncomfortable.

Even married Alison can hold the podium for a while because her husband is infuriating. She had the foresight to marry a narcissistic prick. So Alison gets to tell stories about how Gregory never expresses love, is sexually shut down, and thinks Alison needs to "lose the turkey fat around her neck." And then we go for thirty minutes on how reprehensible that is and how he's a misogynist. I'm telling you right now, if Gregory doesn't take it down a notch, I can't hang out with Alison anymore. That's it. I can't compete on such a high level. Besides the hand holding and hugs, she also never has to pay the check.

The absolute lowest moment for me is when the time arrives for the fateful question: "How often do you and your husband have sex?" I have lost friends with this question. I don't want to. I could plead the Fifth. I mean, why should I have to answer? This is the reality of my life and nothing to be ashamed of. I take a deep breath to summon the strength and spit it out. And then the women gasp and scream like I've confessed that I shot my dog. One of them always slams her fist down on the table; a woman's wineglass once smashed in her hand. I'm sorry! We're hot for each other. Jesus!

I wish there was a way to conjure up some drama without someone getting hurt or procuring an STD. I guess it's just an area of discussion I will have to concede to others. I have to think of myself as the therapist who listens and offers advice but doesn't divulge anything about her own personal life. And I won't get two hundred dollars an hour or remind my friends that I don't take insurance.

Now don't let me mislead you here. I said I love my husband, not that our marriage is perfect. There's a huge difference. Elizabeth Taylor and Richard Burton were passionate for each other but unable to sustain a functional marriage. We have a utilitarian marriage and manage to still maintain the veil of romance. But we fight (which is nonsensical because I am the one who's always right).

———

The question has to be asked: When did a happy marriage become so taboo? Sitcoms depict married life as a bickering couple; he's usually heavy and not very attractive and she's usually too smart and beautiful for him. There's a lot of eye rolling. The couple begrudgingly puts up with each other and a laugh track. Switch to a cable drama: one of them has murdered the other. The bestselling books and music are always slanted toward heartbreak and relationships gone bad. And how would daytime talk shows survive if we couldn't troll for signs of infidelity or enforce paternity tests?

It's embedded in our culture.

The few couples with good marriages I know keep their happiness on the down low. We meet after dusk at nondescript, out-of-the-way joints. Sometimes Brooklyn, sometimes one of our own homes. We close the shades. We make sure nobody sees us holding hands, giggling, or, God forbid, embracing. Otherwise, we gather at one of our homes, where we have the freedom to express our love for our respective companion without ridicule or envy.

So until things in our country change, I will have to become masterful at changing the subject and, in some cases, flat-out lying about the state of my union.

And after one of my girlfriend lunches, I will do my usual—weep (with joy) in the back of the subway about the tenacity and fortitude of my marriage. We'll have family dinner, my husband and I will play Scrabble while the kids do their homework, later we'll make love and fall asleep in each other's arms. And swear to never tell another living soul.

Well, except you the reader.

So if you do have a happy marriage or even an adequate one—KEEP IT TO YOURSELF!

CHAPTER 7

HOLD ON TO YOUR SUMMER

I am having a melancholy summer. Which is not usually the case. Out of all the seasons, I've always loved summer the best.

Summer has come to represent a reprieve from real life. A free pass to be carefree, unkempt, and remiss in returning calls. As my friend Isabel says, "It's making dinner in your bathing suit."

But this summer, something is off. This summer is not unfolding in the predictable, jaunty way. This is the summer of my discontent.

The house is quiet. One daughter is at an all-girls camp

in New Hampshire for seven weeks (her letters say nothing about homesickness or missing us) and the other daughter is living on a boat learning to scuba dive (very homesick and threatening to get herself kicked out of the program). And I am eating a bowl of cereal over the sink and watching Mark Wahlberg movies. My husband has been working around the clock monitoring North Korea as they threaten imminent nuclear attacks. You would think that would be what's making me heavyhearted—end of the world and the decline of human existence. But no, it's not a global apocalypse that has me under the covers; it's more personal. It's about my own apocalypse.

I am on the other side of life. And what is prompting this despondent feeling and holding me back from taking my dog to the beach and collecting scallop shells is the wistful realization that my girls are growing up and I am scrambling to find purpose.

People used to constantly tell me, "Oh, enjoy your children, they grow up so fast." I would roll my eyes. Stupid clichéd musings tossed at me as I pushed my Bugaboo through the park. But it is so true! I know I'm getting older; my one chin hair is completely white now. But my children? They are supposed to run around in retro Strawberry Shortcake bikinis building sandcastles forever!

When I was a little girl, we spent the summer on Cape Cod. There was no television, no computers, and, of course, no social media. We had one rotary phone in the kitchen that almost never rang, and if it did, we knew it was a wrong number and so nobody would ever answer it.

We lived on the gray, splintery wraparound porch. We lay on beach towels and watched my mother snap beans into a ceramic bowl with peace signs on it. Occasionally we would walk down to the Eel River Beach Club for a fire-cracker Popsicle. Once a week we got to pile into our Woody station wagon and go to Tastee-Freez for some soft-serve ice cream. Summers were playing dress up with a musty trunk of old dresses that belonged to my grandmother. Her hats were always infested with spiders. And corn. Lots of corn. Not the hats, the summers. And thoughts. Lots of thoughts.

It's amazing what the brain is capable of when not un-der siege by Twitter, CNN, Instagram, and Snapchat. It's so difficult now for an original thought to squeeze through all the noise. But I can remember lying in a hammock at dusk, pondering what my life would be like. And where my future husband was at that precise moment. At that time it was Lee Majors, and he was shooting *The Six Million Dol-lar Man* at Universal Studios in Hollywood. I can still con-jure the sensation of looking up at the huge elm tree and counting its limbs while gently swinging back and forth. When Lee Majors married Farrah Fawcett I was shocked! Not because they didn't make the perfect couple (made-from-a-factory perfect!), but because she was my doppel-gänger! If I were just a few years older it could have been me! We were practically interchangeable, I just needed to sprout boobs. And sparking white teeth. And long tan legs. And a mane of butter-blonde hair. And sex appeal. That's just bad timing. Years later when he and Farrah divorced, I was over him and had moved on to Warren Beatty. I'm sure it still stings Lee Majors, but I didn't want a man with bionic parts anymore. And with Warren Beatty, it would be just one bionic part.

When I had my children, I knew I wanted to give them the same wistful summer experience. They would know soon enough the rough-and-tumble realities of the world, but while they were little I wanted them to have the chance to lie on a hammock under a big elm tree.

My husband and I are raising our daughters in New York City. That's where my husband's work is, so that is where we live. And it's a fascinating and electrifying town. But I wanted my kids to have grass and sticks and rocks. How can you build a fairy house out of moss and wild mushrooms in a Manhattan apartment? There are trees and rocks in the depths of Central Park, and I recently discovered a waterfall in the north woods near Harlem. But that was just minutes before a fully naked man ran by me.

I was so shocked and traumatized by the image of an unshorn and fuzzy heinie (something I will never be able to unsee) that I texted my husband for help.

"Honey, I'm really scared! A fully naked man just ran by me in the woods and there's nobody around!"

He texted back, "LOL."

Another time, I was alone in our house in Long Island. I really don't like sleeping alone unless the bed is covered in rottweilers. I've seen far too many "the voice is coming from inside the house" films.

The front door was locked. I finished the last pizza crust and was moments from turning off the local news when a report came on that there was a potential rapist on the loose. I was shaking. I grabbed my cell and called my husband. What he could do from a hundred miles away I hadn't thought through.

"Honey! They just said on the news that there's a serial rapist on the loose!"

There was a long pause and then he said matter-of-factly and with a slight chuckle, "You're fine."

Within a couple hours' driving radius of Manhattan, there are a few options. There is north into the Hudson Valley with its bucolic rolling hills and farmland; New Jersey, which offers both surf and turf; and the Hamptons with all its elitist trappings and horrific traffic—but also the Jitney (New Yorkers' version of a Peter Pan bus except with a bathroom, snacks, and a movie). But there is a quaint side of the Hamptons—farm stands, old-fashioned movie theaters, candy stores, and the mighty Atlantic ocean. We are definitely beach people. Even the sight of water relaxes me. We found a sweet little house in the town of East Hampton. My husband was working, I was pregnant, and the house needed some love and tenderness. So I would paint a bathroom around my enormous belly until two in the morning listening to the Grateful Dead and during the day hunt for distressed antiques to add to our roost. I always had Herculean strength at the end of each pregnancy. I moved furniture that would take three husky college boys to haul. Instead of a chic, straw summer bag, I toted around a toolbox.

And then the babies came. I would hold them tightly as their chubby little legs swished around the surface of the pool. Every day was sandy toes and nontoxic paint all over the backyard, the slate patio, and, in some spots, the kitchen walls. We would eat steamers drenched in butter on a quilt in the yard and lick ice-cream cones before the tops fell off (usually onto my sandals).

The girls got bigger, and we moved and the activities became more active. We discovered huge round rocks and painted pig faces and fish on them. We collected pieces of shells and searched for sea glass. Even though I wasn't pregnant I still stayed up until two in the morning painting bathrooms and listening to the Grateful Dead.

We would meet up with family friends for clambakes or capture the flag . . . For a few years Fourth of July was in our yard. I would bake way too many red, white, and blue cupcakes and cheesecakes and watch the kids run around with sparklers and cannonball into the pool. There were magical nights when my daughters and their friends, adorned in sundresses, fairy wings, and bare feet, would frolic in the grass and bushes collecting fireflies in mason jars. I mean, is that a great Verizon Wireless commercial or what?

It was during their young years that I discovered crabbing. Or should I say, the art of crabbing. Not just anyone can throw a string attached to a chicken wing and haul in dinner for six people! My girls would sit under a beach umbrella with apple slices and watch their daft mother knee-deep in the bay trying to outsmart crustaceans. But for me those days were euphoric. I lived in ripped jeans and carried my babies from sand to water and home for crafts. I didn't have a cell phone and I don't remember watching anything on TV except *The Sopranos*. I was mostly singing "The wheels on the bus" and making the girls squeal while I showed them how to put a lobster to sleep by rubbing its belly. And the exhaustion at the end of the day! I would collapse with kids and dogs all over me on the bed, everyone smelling like the sea and vanilla ice cream. It was pure bliss.

Today, I am alone in the house. My daughters' childhood dogs have gone to heaven, a place in the clouds made of bologna and pork chops or wherever they go to in the afterlife. And we have two new canines. They are out in the yard yelping at what they think is a deer but is actually a feral cat that lives in the brambles. In the house there's nothing more to paint, hammer, or strip. I can see faint green stains on the sofa from many summers ago when my kids tried to tie-dye all the furniture. There is a plate of homemade chewy molasses cookies on the counter that I now bake by habit. But it's only me who will eat them. And our hound dog whose tongue seems to swipe the counter. I caress the smooth stones we painted, stare at the huge, light blue jars of shells we have collected over the years. All remnants, all relics of joyful afternoons.

So with this summer has come the realization that those serene and breezy days are gone. Yes, there are different days to come. There will be awkward walks with their new boyfriends and evening dinners to advise on career choices. But they will never Benjamin Button back to the cherubs who used to run around naked in the sprinkler or cover themselves in glue and glitter.

They did grow up too fast. But I have to remind myself that they are still growing and blossoming into the amazing adults they will soon become. And I can revel in every minute of it. I will hug them, squeeze them, and smell them. I will smooth their hair and hold their hands as we sit down to dinner every night. I will know them, appreciate them, and love them.

My elm tree now is in the form of two beautiful girls and I will lie with them and ponder and not allow the noise of the outside world to distract and intrude. I will hold them tight as we rock back and forth. And explain to them who Lee Majors is.

My children, I have discovered, log the time for me.

When I was young, time was irrelevant. Summers were endless and the possibilities were infinite. But now, standing in my kitchen in a still house, wondering if it's too depressing to go to the farm stand and buy one ear of corn, I realize that this is it. My life will not change that much, mostly because it's more than half over.

Last night I had one of the most vivid dreams I've ever had (or at least ever remembered). In the dream I was shooting a movie in London, a period piece. The setting was the 1700s and I was an American patriot in England, on a journey with my parents. In the film, I was set to marry a boy back in Boston I didn't love. And during the course of the film I fell in love with the son of a British farmer. The dream was in Technicolor and I could virtually smell the sawdust from the set. The kind of dream that when you're immersed in it, your brain truly believes it is your reality. I could feel the tight corset (probably because my pajamas pants were too tight) and the sweat from running through the fields with my lover (played by the lead in the film *Kingsman*), which was probably sweat from perimenopause. There was also a very intense love scene. My body looked milky white and svelte. And those were definitely not my boobs (yes, I repeat, this was a dream).

I woke up to the annoying buzz of my iPhone alarm. It took me a minute to convince myself that I wasn't tangled up with my lover in a hayloft, but alone on a Posturepedic mattress in Manhattan. I was profoundly depressed at the idea of never being, let alone playing, a young damsel in distress. And that any youthful adventures would be relegated to nocturnal unconsciousness.

And as I patted on my glycolic pads and sunscreen, it hit me. My life wasn't over because I had hit a certain number. If I wanted to, I could make love in a haystack—I mean, ouch! and I don't necessarily need a stalk of wheat up my ass, but I could! I was still the patriot girl, just in mom jeans and Tretorns. And I had married the love of my life . . . Granted, he's not the British actor in *Kingsman* (who, let's be honest, could be my son), but a much more suitable, swarthy Greek soul mate. With my superficial self-esteem, a much younger lover would leave me plastic surgery bills that would have me mortgaging the house.

So perhaps I shouldn't dissect the dream as it pertains to an unfulfilled life, but view it as simply what it was—a middle-aged woman's sex dream! Yes, women don't dream porn; there is a plot which is unveiled in three acts. And often a sequel.

What I'm really talking about is the acceptance of life in the present and a need for more turtlenecks. I don't need to press pause and mourn the past; I simply need to cultivate an enlightened excitement for the future.

Plus, there's always grandchildren. . . . Bring on the fairy wings and glitter!

CHAPTER 8

PRETTY FUNNY

I'm not sure I would have made it through adolescence if social media existed in my rather desperate, overweight high school years. I body-shamed myself enough, I didn't need the hormonally engorged boys to tell me I was not f***able enough. And the bikini shots that plaster Instagram now? I wouldn't have stood a chance, even with Photoshop.

I wasn't a cheerleader, so there was nothing to bring it on. I wasn't a jock—well, I am a WASP, so I played mediocre tennis and skied well enough to be invited on other people's trips. But I found myself in the 1980s version of having to identify myself. Rather plump, Caucasian, nondescript female.

I believe it was Amy Schumer who said that when she first started doing stand-up, she realized it was way better being funny than being pretty. I completely agree. I had that epiphany doing a Christopher Durang play in high school. It was meant to be a dramatic tour de force; I was playing an introverted cello player. But in the beginning of the second act I spread my legs wide to make room for the cello and it was the most blatant sexual gesture, yet my expression was completely nonchalant. The audience broke out in uproarious laughter. I remember the feeling perfectly, a rush of elation that rippled through my body, as if it's frozen in time. It's what I imagine it's like to walk on the moon, win an Olympic gold medal, have a real orgasm. . . . For me, it was better than being crowned prom queen. Or monarch of the British empire for that matter.

From that night forward, I chose funny over pretty. In fact, I lost interest in trying to compete in the gorgeous arena. Don't get me wrong, I didn't become Leonardo DiCaprio in *The Revenant*; I still shaved my legs once a week and exfoliated, I just didn't put all my chips down on my exterior.

My first love was a drop-your-pencil James Spader (circa *Pretty in Pink*) Harvard-bound seventeen-year-old boy. I was a slightly overweight teenager with thin hair and no fashion sense. Unless you consider Laura Ashley flannel turtleneck dresses with knee socks and clogs chic. And to spare you the banal details of our courtship and cut to the chase: I got the guy. Not so much because I told the joke, but because I told and got the joke. I could make him laugh by making simple observations of our daily adolescent life. Oh, and I could act out all of the parts in *Jesus Christ Superstar*!

As I got older, I honed my comedic skills. I had a friend who was completely fixated with the exterior. She would use a safety pin to separate each lash after she applied mascara, ate celery by the bushel, and spent Friday nights at home applying olive oil to her hair and watching *Knots Landing* in a face mask. As much as I was in awe of her laborious beauty routines, I knew it was ultimately a mug's game. Not because a large percentage of her waking hours was consumed by blemish hunting, but because no other facet of herself ever had the chance to develop. Sure, she looked amazing in a bohemian dress and gladiator sandals, but when she pulled her chair up to the table, that was all there was. I would watch the gazes that were initially so focused on her slowly turn away. And whereas I was initially met with pleasantries, it was my off-color stories that eventually drew in those gazes.

And so my confidence grew. And like any muscle, that was the one I worked and massaged. At fifty-two, my body is begging me to work out the other muscles, but my butt has a mind of her own.

In full disclosure, I am now a middle-aged woman who could use an hour a day on the treadmill and some baby

Botox; there is a balance. But as I witness my friends frantically squating, lunging, planking, and injecting, I am confident that my sense of humor will never lose its elasticity or require human growth hormones. It will always be my strength, my shield, my Kardashian lips. Listen, beauty fades; a good political joke never does. And if you ask me if I could come back in another life, would it be as either Brigitte Bardot or Phyllis Diller? Phyllis Diller all the way, baby!

So it's particularly fascinating to now have teenage girls who are obsessive about contouring cheekbones, Kyle Jenner's lip gloss line, and DIY avocado face masks. The other day I found them in the kitchen stirring up Elmer's glue and charcoal, which they then brushed on their faces for a few hours until it almost peeled the first few layers of their skin off. "You already have perfect skin! And stop trying to look younger, you are twelve and fifteen! You are already younger! You want infant skin?" Gotta be pretty pretty pretty pretty! And it's nearly impossible to compete against the infinitude of wannabe models on social media. My daughters actually DM (direct message, Mom) these women for tips on becoming one of the pillars of beautification. I walk around our home repeating my mantra, "It's much cooler to be an attractive biochemist," which is always met by an eye roll or a whisper, "No it's not."

But the moment I knew I was fighting a losing battle was on a rainy night in September. In our house bedtime takes an hour. First my husband and I have to herd our children like sheep to give up their phones, put on pajamas, and brush their teeth. That takes five minutes. The next fifty-five minutes are spent on frivolous, pointless beauty regimens. My twelve-year-old does not need retinol on her forehead or a blemish strip taped across her nose. And my fifteen-year-old has more product layering and steps than a renovation of a historic house. What is so hysterical to me is that these products all contradict one another. The organic face oil is then taken off with an anti-oil astringent followed by a moisturizing oil-based face cream. They'd have better results scrubbing my stainless-steel utensils with silver polish. After they have put their youthful epidermis through a schizophrenic series of punishments, they kiss us good night and hibernate in their caves of Polaroid selfies and spewed homework binders. That night, our youngest bounced up in her fluffy onesie covered in rainbow-colored doughnuts, gave us each a quick peck on the cheek, and skipped away with a faint "Love you!" And then entered our eldest with shiny cheeks (I assumed maybe car wax) and two plastic clips on her nose. They looked like strange surgical tools. "What the hell is on your nose?" I laughed. "They're Japanese nose shapers. I ordered them off Amazon," she answered. My husband looked at her in curious horror. "They're WHAT?" In full adolescent swing, she stared at us as if she could smell our idiocy. "It's a nose uplifting, shaping bridge straightener.

It works without having to have plastic surgery!" Silence. Both my husband and I were furiously scrambling to find the words to end her ethnic cleansing. So I just ripped the ridiculous plastic toys off her face. "You have a wonderful, beautiful Greek nose that defines you! If you ever put these potato-chip clippers back on your schnoz, I'm going to show up at your parent-teacher conference in a gold bikini and roller skates." My Lord, what happened to interesting, unique features? Frida Kahlo would be cyberbullied for that unibrow today. Why do women scrutinize the minutiae and not the big picture? This episode disturbed me as I fear having daughters who are punishing their authentic, unique Mediterranean skin. And self-esteem. And it's already so stressful growing up in a celebrity-obsessed social media world. There's something liberating in not caring. Although my poor husband might disagree a little. . . .

A couple of weeks later my eldest came home from school with her dirty hair in a top knot, no hint of makeup, and no sign of self-mutilation over a blackhead. She had come from a heated debate in her history class about sexual harassment, race, and the plight of women. She couldn't stop talking and gesticulating. She was all fired up. "Sexual harassment is just a symptom of a much larger problem. It's about women and power, women in the boardroom, women getting equal pay . . . the only thing men can process and be responsible for now is the harassment because of evidence and strong voices, but so much more needs to transpire for us to even begin to feel equal!" I yanked the backpack off her shoulders and gave her a big squeeze. "When you use your mind like that and get excited about your own thoughts and beliefs? THAT is beautiful and stunning and awesome!" She kissed me and we kept hugging. After a pause she said, "Can I whiten my teeth?"

PART II

CAUTIONARY TALES

I'VE SEEN THINGS, AND THAT'S ALMOST THE SAME
AS DOING THEM.

—LORETTA LYNN

CHAPTER 9

LESSONS FROM A MOVIE STAR

A kind and honest man taught me a great lesson about misdirected love. He is one of our great actors, and even though he deserves total recognition for the life lesson he imparted to me, the details of his life are not mine to tell . . . and my editor won't even let me say what his name rhymes with.

I was a young actress—not a nubile ingenue, but a twenty-three-year-old recklessly driving around Los Angeles from one audition to another in a dilapidated Ford Fiesta, sometimes changing outfits while my knees gripped the steering wheel. My seat was littered with sandwich halves, old ginger ale cans, tattered scripts, and (don't judge, it was cool at the time) empty packs of Marlboro Lights. What a vision. If my husband had bumped into me back then, he would have run the other way and lathered any sliver of exposed skin with Purell.

I finally had a respectable audition. Or as my mother called them, tryouts. It was in a real office building with a receptionist, where you needed a parking pass and not an empty hangar in the San Fernando Valley that either housed illegal semiautomatic weapons or shot porn on Beta. My hands weren't shaking. I didn't fiddle with my tight skirt. And I didn't look down at my shoes the whole time like a nun being scolded. And I actually heard laughter instead of the sounds of the casting people chomping on their Big Macs while they riffled through other head shots.

I received a callback. The director was a jolly Brit who appreciated my sense of humor. And I will love him forever for it. In fact, I will love all British people for it.

When I got the call from my agent that I had booked the movie, I burst into tears. Not tears of sadness but rather tears of joy that my parents were wrong about me. I steeled myself through costume fittings, a table read, makeup tests; it was all so Hollywood. Or what I perceived Hollywood to be.

Now, my career has been eclectic, to say the least. I've acted in drama, comedy, film, TV, digital, everything but porn. (Never say never.) I write scripts and books. I do public speaking and emcee charity events. And not once in my illustrious (I just wanted to use that word) career have I been asked to dress provocatively. More specifically, in lingerie. I have always been the stable friend, bitchy fiancée, or neurotic girlfriend. My wardrobe fittings consist of tightening the backs of suits, finding a lower heel, and padding my bra. Always padding my bra.

With one notable exception: For one of my scenes in this particular movie, I was fitted in a lacy, powder-blue teddy. It was attached to a garter belt and sheer stockings. It was the most naked I had ever been (forget on-screen, in life). In the film I played the main character's fiancée who surprises her out-of-town beau with an unexpected visit just as he's falling in love with a gorgeous waitress. I was beyond self-conscious. I walked through the set like a five-year-old in heels, like a colt learning to walk. I had to pass all the PAs and key grips, my buttocks on display like banana cream pies at a county fair. It's worth adding that until this point, the closest thing to a love scene on my résumé was when I had to kiss a guy in my acting class. (He had halitosis and used his tongue.)

The director huddled with me and the leading man about the scene. It was difficult to peel my eyes off the movie star. I'd seen so many of his films and here I was standing next to him in the flesh, exposing my flesh. And I had to play up the sexiness. We were about to shoot the scene wherein his character had fallen out of love with me and the true object of his affections was moments away from entering the room. So I needed to make the situation even more tense. The humor being the build of his angelic lady friend finding us in a compromising position. Suffice it to say, he hadn't told this lovely woman (played by one of the sexiest starlets in Hollywood) that he was engaged.

And action! "Surprise," I screamed and threw myself upon him, my legs pythoned around his middle. He tried to push me away, which only made me clamp on more fiercely. Remember the film *20,000 Leagues Under the Sea*? When the giant squid tries to envelop the ship? That was me. As soon as the director would yell cut, we would linger around craft service nibbling on brownie bits or use the bathroom. About twenty minutes later, we would start up again.

We must have done twenty different takes of me with my tongue licking the side of his face and his palms secured on my breasts. I'm mortified to recall that I actually bit one of his nipples. We were as intimate as I had been with any of my past (committed) boyfriends. And when you are kissing and fondling someone, physical and (for me at least) involuntary emotional responses follow. That's just how the brain and the private parts communicate and transmit feelings. And my costar certainly had a "reaction" as well, one that kept hitting my hip bone.

At the end of the shooting day, I changed into my sweatpants and tattered T-shirt and headed back to my modest dwelling for cereal and a new episode of *ER*. I thought about what had transpired on the set that day and decided that I couldn't be alone in my feelings; the leading man clearly was falling for me. True, he was a great actor, but there was no way he could have been faking it; the body never lies. We had become lost in each other and it was as if there were no cameras, lights, or makeup people around us; we were alone in a hotel room in the desert (set). And we had fallen in love. How would I manage the rest of the shoot? Should we announce ourselves as a new couple or do our best to keep it on the down low? And was I ready to become a famous Hollywood couple thrown into the den of tabloid magazines and talk-show fodder? This was way before Brangelina, so we would have been the first, we would have been . . . oops, almost gave him away!

I couldn't sleep that night. My life was about to change. For the better (not that it would take much). He and I would make films together, travel the world, maybe even start a band? I slipped into the hair and makeup trailer well before my call so I would look dewy and fresh when he arrived on set. I considered knocking on his Gulfstream and surprising him, maybe a passionate make-out session before he shot that boring monologue-to-a-cop scene. But that wouldn't be fair to him. He couldn't go recite serious prose postcoital and with a smirk plastered on his face. I refrained and made a reservation at a posh Asian fusion restaurant for us that evening.

I spent most of the morning in my kennel cage of a

dressing room reading magazines and messing up the *New York Times* crossword puzzle. I clipped my toenails and excavated my face for pimples like a caffeinated, anxious teenager. I decided we should talk about the future, our status, and just general plans. I didn't even know what religion he was. Or if he had food allergies! Suddenly, there was a bang on my flimsy door and a nondescript production assistant peeked his head in, wearing his headset with such pride, you would have thought he was Chance the Rapper on tour. "We're at lunch!" he exclaimed before squawking into his walkie-talkie. It was time to share a burrito out of a truck with my future husband.

The leading man sat alone at one of the long plastic tables set up for the cast and crew. Usually the stars eat in their private quarters with their glam squad and assistants, but not my love. He was one of the people, like Karl Marx or Bernie Sanders. He was quietly munching on a spinach salad, lost in a script. I placed my tray down directly across from him. He looked up, smiled, and went back to reading.

I didn't expect a proposal, but I was confused by his lack of enthusiasm after the previous lustful day. "Can I ask you a question?" I asked softly.

He nonchalantly answered, without looking up, "Sure . . . shoot!"

"What are we? I mean, what's going on with us?"

The leading man stared at me as if I'd just confessed to a hit-and-run.

"I'm not sure . . . what do you mean . . ." he stuttered.

"Well . . . yesterday . . . it was so heated . . . obviously we both were feeling . . . aren't we, you know, a thing?"

He almost vomited spinach and bacon bits. And then gingerly pushed away his script like he was preparing to reason with a serial killer.

"Listen, you gotta understand this world. I learned a lesson a long time ago about this industry. It's all make-believe, Ali." What the hell was he saying? "When the director yells cut, it's over. All of it. Suddenly, you're no longer fighting a dragon or loving the person you're kissing or in bed with. It's a surreal job we have."

This was not a job! This was a life we were going to build together! What did dragons have to do with how many children we would have?

"I've done many love scenes with some of the most beautiful women in the world and if I allowed myself to fall in love with all of them, well, I'd bounce from one shallow sexcapade to another. You have to be able to draw the line between what's real and not real."

He was breaking up with me. This had to be one of my top short-lived relationships, less than twenty-four hours. A record, actually.

I stared down at my Converse high-tops. "I get it. It just gets confusing, you know? I've never done any kind of kissing or even a love scene."

He smiled so nicely. "I did an independent movie years

ago. It was never distributed. But the female lead was an actress named [Don't be angry, I can't tell you her real name! Again, it's his story to tell, not mine. I'm just doing the lesson part.] Jenna."

My eyes widened. "Jenna Rubin? Oh my God! I didn't know you two did a film together."

"We did. A very sexy movie where we shared an uncontrollable passion. She played a prostitute and I was a gritty cop from the Bronx who saved her from being sold to an Arab prince—"

"I would have loved that movie," I interrupted.

"And a couple weeks into shooting I realized that we weren't playacting anymore and our love scenes were actual love scenes. And three weeks after we wrapped I was sitting in a hotel room in Beverly Hills with Jenna Rubin and I thought, What the hell have I done!"

My hand covered my mouth. "She's nuts, right?"

The leading man gave me a penetrating look as if to bring the whole story home. "I left my wife and kids for her. I blew up my life for a hollow fantasy. It took me years to get back with my wife. I was a fool."

I nodded. "Wow."

"Don't be a fool, Ali."

That humid afternoon in Los Angeles saved me years of heartache and therapy. Well, not therapy; there was a plethora of other issues to chew on. But this man, this grown-up, could have easily taken advantage of the situation. I was there for the plucking. But he chose to share a very private story in the hopes that I would never make the same mistake. And I haven't. Oh, I've made a million other mistakes, but I never again became unzipped when it came to infatuation. And I learned the difference between real and make-believe. (Only at work, though.)

Jenna Rubin has kept the tabloids flush with her marriages, affairs, and subsequent divorces. And even though she's a sexy (although long in the tooth now) celebrity, when I catch her on the cover of an *OK!* or *In Touch* in CVS, I can't help but exhale and think, "Could have been me, could have been me."

For those of you in entertainment—don't confuse the fairy-tale nature of being on a set with truth. And that includes reality shows. Same rules apply outside of entertainment. You're not really in love with your son's lacrosse coach. You're not going to run off to Mustique with him and live in a straw hut making love and eating banana bread all day. Don't project your fantasies onto other people. You will be disappointed. As the children's book states, "Everybody farts."

CHAPTER 10

PEKA GONE

I have said this many times before: As much as I love the film *Love Story*, Erich Segal's infamous line "Love means never having to say you're sorry" is a complete falsehood. As is the idea that you would find two people that beautiful at Harvard University.

I usually blame unwarranted and irritable behavior on hormones or lack of sleep. But occasionally it's just a matter of pure, unmitigated anger. It is imperative, however, that after you give the finger to someone in the school carpool lane (who turns out to be the principal) or snap at your husband about not being appreciative enough (as he's carrying up a breakfast tray with the *New York Times*), you apologize. Nothing, not pride, alcohol, or arrogance, should stop you. In fact, even if you believe you did nothing wrong, just apologize. Trust me.

We were living in Washington, D.C., when I had my second baby and it was clear I needed help. And sleep. One of the greatest gifts a mother can receive is an extra pair of hands—whether they belong to one's mother, sister, friend, or employee. My extra hands came in the form of a petite Indian woman named Peka.

Peka was always smiling. Whether she had her dentures in or not. And she was always amenable to any plan.

"Peka, grab your boots we're going to jump in puddles!"

"Okay!" Big smile.

"Peka, we're having a princess party, can you help me bake a five-tier light blue Cinderella cake?"

"Okay!" Big smile.

"Peka, we've just robbed the Citibank near the mall, start the car, grab the fake passports, and head to the airport."

"Okay!" Big smile.

Peka played the lottery every single day. And didn't much care for "creative" food (as she called my cooking). Her most precious belongings were a Crock-Pot (always filled with warm rice) and a flat-screen TV. Her favorite show was *Dancing with the Stars*. She would scream at the judges the way the Patriots' coach yells at the refs. For her those scores were life and death for the dancers. And whenever the judge named Bruno would gyrate and convulse over a contestant, Peka would clap her hands and laugh, "He's so crazy man!"

Peka was my wife for four years. We would swap the girls like we were running a relay race. If this one needed a nap, Peka would put her down and read *US Weekly* while I took the other to music class. When I came home, it was my turn to catch up on *The Wire*. I told her everything. When you spend that much time with someone—a colleague, life partner, jailmate, sous chef—they are compelled to listen to your stories, thoughts, plans, dreams, and fears . . . whether they like it or not. Peka loved to give me her thoughts about the other mothers in the play group. Who she liked, who had "evil in her eyes," and who was just one "sad lady."

Very few people could make me laugh like Peka did. She once told me what a spiteful temper she'd had as a child; every time she was insolent to her mother, her mother punished Peka by cutting off all her hair. So defiant Peka spent most of her time hiding up in papaya trees.

Sometimes she made me laugh unintentionally. If I went for a walk, she would clap and say, "Oh Mommy! Yes! You keep walking and no more fat fat!" as she rubbed my belly and waist. Or when I would have to go to a black-tie event with my husband and so would wear makeup and actually blow out my hair: "Oh Mommy . . . yes, yes, makeup much better for you!" She never meant to be unkind; in her mind, honesty was the greatest compliment.

And then we moved to Manhattan. And Peka came, too. I didn't realize the hurdles you had to jump over in order to buy an apartment. On the island of Manhattan in the 1500s, you threw down a few rabbit skins and some chunks of gold and you were given a timber-framed house with a thatched roof. But the folks on New York City co-op boards today no longer appear to be interested in straightforward, fair trades. To me it's black and white. You have the money, the apartment is for sale, you give them a check, they give you a set of keys. Unfortunately, it's not that easy. Ask Madonna.

Our board interview felt like a parole hearing. My husband and I sat across from four members and a fruit and cheese plate. Having never auditioned to live in a building before, I was very self-conscious. I hesitated to reach for the Brie. I just knew it was a trap. Yet I didn't want to be unappreciative, so I chewed on a cracker. But I wanted a heap of the gooey cheese so bad. We were asked very practical questions about how much entertaining we did (I assured them that we limited the Ecstasy parties to Tuesdays and Thursdays and that Bon Jovi would only jam on Christian holidays). And they asked what my husband's salary was. Nothing personal about that. I assumed the next step was for them to swab our mouths.

One of the women eyed me like she knew I was the type of person who stole umbrellas from hotels. Let's call her Mrs. Gaynor. She was a dead ringer for Lady Bird Johnson, with a coif so lacquered I was confident she would never suffer a concussion. A confident woman who took pride in her appearance and her bold lipstick color choice. A lady who takes a brisk walk outside whenever she needs to pass gas.

Thank God I didn't eat the cheese, because we were accepted. Accepted to live in an apartment we were paying for. Go figure.

———

Apartment living is a curious thing. You share a building with a group of strangers, so you're kind of roommates—or, at the very least, buildingmates. But you're not sharing a fridge or fighting over who's responsible for the cigarette burn on the couch. And yet you rub elbows with your neighbors almost every day. Whenever the elevator door opens I hold my breath waiting to see which cast of characters I will share a ride with. Or if I'm with our dogs, which person they will bark at before shoving their snouts into the person's crotch. It's usually a polite hello and then an awkward silence until we reach the cacophony of the lobby and street ahead.

On the rare occasion it was Mrs. Gaynor, dressed to the nines and smelling like Bulgari perfume. An elegant woman who was always very complimentary, even when my hair was wet, I had the flu, and I looked like death. It bears mentioning that she is a formidable woman; even as she doled out the insincere flattery, you could practically see the thought bubble over her head: "Oh, if I had an afternoon I could fix this mess of a girl up!" That thought's probably in many people's bubble. Lord knows it's been hovering over my mother's head for forty years.

Peka had helped Mrs. Gaynor hire a new housekeeper. A friend named Tamar, who lived near Peka in the Bronx. Mrs. Gaynor was so grateful to Peka for finding such "a good girl" to help her.

I had been in Los Angeles for a few days pitching original ideas (if they're not attached to the Marvel franchise, they don't have a shot). I wearily walked into our lobby dragging a Tumi suitcase with only one wheel behind me. All I wanted was a bath and a pint of coffee Häagen-Dazs. But I would have settled for a whore's bath and a bowl of cornflakes.

Just as I hit the elevator button, our super approached me with a concerned look on his face. My first thought was: Did I leave the toaster on? And then the dreaded: We have roaches.

"We have a situation," he announced, as portentous as Harrison Ford in the movie *Air Force One*.

Speaking in a hushed whisper, he filled me in. In a plotline worthy of an episode of *Scandal*, Peka had imploded. Apparently, Tamar had written on her Facebook page that Peka had bedbugs. Now, bedbugs aren't high on anyone's wish list, but to Peka such an accusation amounted to defamation of character. If you had bedbugs, then you were a dirty person. (Full disclosure: I got bedbugs once from a bed-and-breakfast in Northern California. I googled bedbugs and it suggested microwaving your clothing. So I did. But Google never said for how long. After four minutes my pajamas ignited and the microwave blew up.) Anyway, for Peka this was a declaration of war. She started taking the back stairs up to the Gaynors' apartment to confront and chastise Tamar. This had been going on for some time: Unbeknownst to us, our super had taken Peka aside a few times over the past weeks to explain the rules of trespassing and breaking and entering.

"I told her, she can't just walk into an apartment and start bitch-slapping someone working there! These are all separate homes." And as fate would have it, Mrs. Gaynor entered the elevator at the exact time Peka was taking our incontinent dachshund out to pee. (Well, out for fresh air; she only pees inside the apartment, on whichever carpet will absorb the most urine.) In that moment Peka erupted in fireworks of fury. She started yelling at Mrs. Gaynor about Tamar and bedbugs and using language that caused Mrs. Gaynor to have heart palpitations. By the time the door opened in the lobby, Peka was still inflamed, Mrs. Gaynor was experiencing cardiac arrest, and the dachshund had peed all over the elevator rug.

All this was regaled to me as I was propping up my broken wheelie bag, operating on little sleep and a bag of Pop Chips. Mrs. Gaynor had gone to her daughter-in-law's to recover and Peka was upstairs in the apartment. I needed a shrink, a lawyer, and a fistful of antianxiety medication.

When I entered the apartment Peka was making tea.

"Oh Mommy! You are back from Hollywood! Maybe you became a big star?" She giggled.

I turned off the whistling kettle and brought Peka to the living room. "You need to immediately write a letter to Mrs. Gaynor and apologize."

Peka stood up. "No! She apologize to me!"

"Peka, listen to me, she is on the board of the building and you screamed obscenities in her face and almost caused her to have a heart attack. I'm trying to save your job! Write the woman a letter and say you are very sorry. I will help you."

"I no write anyone a letter. She needs to write me a letter."

Clearly Peka did not comprehend the magnitude of the situation.

My husband called. He had been talking to the building management company. They were filing a restraining order against Peka. Either she left or we had to.

I pleaded with her again. But her refrain remained the same: "She say sorry to me! And Tamar say sorry on Facebook!"

There was no reasoning with her. I was starting to understand why her mother had resorted to cutting her hair off. My mother suggested sending her to a psychiatric facility for anger management. And after the kind of stand-off

I dimly recall from my American Civil War history class, we came to an impasse. Peka refused to make an apology and the building refused entry.

It was heartbreaking for our family to say good-bye to Peka. We did manage to secure her a job with friends who have folded her into their family seamlessly. And so far no devil dancing.

And the one thing my husband and I still repeat to each other as we're putting on pajamas or waiting for our car in the garage: All she had to do was apologize. . . . It was a lesson that has afforded me long-lasting relationships, semiregular employment, and long hair. And by the way, at the end of *Love Story* when Oliver Barrett III apologizes to his son (Ryan O'Neal)? He should just have accepted it and moved on! That is what Jenny (Ali MacGraw) would have wanted him to do!

CHAPTER 11

HOT BABYSITTER

can't believe I even have to make this point, but DO NOT HIRE A HOT BABYSITTER! I know that in voicing such an opinion I'm breaking some affirmative action law and nubile women with rock'n bods are going to sue me, but come on! I don't care that she (in a thong bikini) taught your child to swim or makes the most incredible gluten-free carrot muffins; a hot babysitter is a distraction for every person in the family. Yes, even the dog.

If you are in the market for a caregiver, chances are your body has been through a raging nine-month war. Yes, you have created human life blah blah blah, but your skin has been stretched out like a rubber band—without contracting back. And there is either a C-section scar that suggests a shark attack or your vagina has gone through its own battle of Waterloo, with the scars to prove it. So already you're at a disadvantage because you have the self-esteem of a hairless cat. Why would you employ (yes, pay money to) an improved, souped-up version of you and have her promenade around your house?

Let's play this out . . . there she is, let's call her Sofia (as in Vergara, or Loren if you're my dad). You're wearing the Lanz nightgown your mother gave you when you were in the hospital for an appendectomy during college. It's commodious and unrestricted, with a faded bluebell flower pattern. It's somewhat tattered and has tiny spittle stains that even the triple-action stain remover Shout can't get out. You're barefoot, you haven't had a pedicure for six months (so your toenails look like a Cambodian priest's), and your hair is two distinct colors—your authentic dishwater brown and the remnants of blond highlights. You look like the mug shot of a meth addict.

Good news, though—there's still a hunk of two-day-old coffee-cake crumble on the counter, so you break off a wedge and shove it in your mouth. Enter Sofia. Sofia is wearing Daisy Duke jean shorts that don't quite manage to contain her perfectly shaped buttocks, a tank top, and flip-flops. She has had a pedicure (Ballet Slippers is the name of the polish), which complements the baby rose tattoo on her ankle; her hair is surferlike tossed and tangled; and she looks spray-tanned, but she's not—she just "tans easily and evenly, probably from her days as a lifeguard." Coffee-cake crumbs spill down your front. The nightgown is now a circus tent that hides the house of horrors underneath. And she should be walking the Calvin Klein show during fashion week. You offer her a fistful of cake; she passes. She just had an acai bowl (whatever the hell that is). And slowly your self-worth, when challenged with the nubile nymph that, like a wrecking ball, has entered your life, plummets to a new low. You can just detect her lace G-string peeking out of the waistband of her low-slung (size 24) shorts. And you're still using maxi pads from your episiotomy.

You can't compete, so decide to join. Another bad idea. You cannot be girlfriends with your babysitter. There's no magical osmosis process by which through logging time with her you suddenly absorb all her physical traits and can share clothes. Even if you kill her, peel off her skin, glue it on your own face like a Hannibal Lector mask—you will never have her supple, luminescent glow.

No, don't try to bond by exercising together. Do you really want to go to spin class with Sofia? Sofia could teach that class, and your doctor warned you that you have the breathing capacity of a sixty-five-year-old woman. There's no being gal pals with Sofia. Your girlfriends don't look like her. Or at least they shouldn't.

Enter the husband (or wife). He (or she) is loving, devoted, oozing with integrity. (From now on I'm just going to use the masculine pronoun, but you can insert whatever

pronoun works for your scenario, except for maybe "we.")
The best-case scenario: He does nothing, but maybe he
brushes against her when loading the stroller into the mini-
van. He appreciates that she's an attractive woman, but
nothing more. Water, water everywhere, but not a drop to
drink. But in the back of your mind, lurking in that dark,
anxious spot, you have to wonder if he has ever thought
about her in a lascivious way. When he was alone. Or even
with you! Repeatedly. He is a man, after all. And don't kid
yourself that you have a better personality—she laughs at
everything he says. For God's sake, Jude Law was engaged
to Sienna Miller and he cheated on *her* with the nanny.

I'm not saying that all men will cheat with the babysitter! But if you were on a diet, would you hang out in a bakery? And by the way, I have two friends whose husbands
slept with the babysitter. So if I know two friends, well,
you can do the math. . . .

And let me be brutally honest here—and I'm sure MIT
and the Harvard psychology department can back me up
on this: Children respond more favorably to a fetching
female. According to an expert I saw on CNN, "Babies
respond more positively to attractive, symmetrical faces."
If my daughters could have, they would have arranged
babysitter cattle calls, complete with head shots. Whenever
they met a pretty twentysomething woman, they would
beg me to hire her.

So you're even more of an insomniac because not only

are you tormented by the idea of your husband and the nanny, but now your child is enamored of her and her ethereal exquisiteness.

———

Here's another: you're in your jersey stretch pants and one of your husband's button-downs sanitizing the house with organic melon-scented spray, when the baby wakes from its nap and starts crying. You rush in to hold that little dumpling that personifies every cell of love you possess . . . and the baby keeps crying. And crying. Sofia comes in with her blinding-white teeth, smelling like St. Bart's, and caresses the baby's cheek. The baby stops crying and starts cooing. Sofia sings Celine Dion's "My Heart Will Go On" and the baby smiles. And you secretly hope Sofia won't attempt to breastfeed while you're at CVS buying stool softeners and *People* magazine.

You, your husband, the baby, and Sofia are all parading around the park. You're a little sweaty and your yoga pants, although soft, can't muffle the chafing sound your thighs make as you walk. You stop at the water fountain. Next to you are two skeletal women in workout gear. They clock Sofia pushing the stroller alongside your dashing husband.

"What a gorgeous family," one says.

"She looks amazing," says the other.

"I can see why he fell in love with her!"

You race back to the group and grab your husband's

hand tightly, seriously entertaining the idea of pulling down your pants and peeing in a circle around his feet.

You have become an insecure mess. And nothing turns a spouse off more than a clingy, accusatory female who has traded in self-maintenance for Carvel Cookie Puss ice cream cakes. It's like you're pushing him into Sofia's ample bosom. Daddy and baby are drawn to Sofia. And the final straw: Your mangy mutt with one eye you rescued from a kill shelter who is terrified of everyone? Will now only eat if Sofia lies down next to him on the floor. In a sexy pose. You have become a ghost in your own home.

It's Sofia's day off, and your husband has taken the child to Baby Einstein class. You've decided, inspired by an old issue of *O, The Oprah Magazine*, to take your life in your hands. You are going to be your best you! You peruse the computer for a nearby Pilates class. Or a pottery class. Whatever works with your schedule. And suddenly you spot an untitled file. The other files have names—Taxes, Vacation, fantasy football, Résumé, Birth Video—but this one is blank. Now, if at this point you log off and go for a ten-mile run, you are not a human being. But if you're like me, you click on the file icon. Let curiosity kill the cat. The cat would probably only love Sofia anyway.

Time stops. As does your pulse for a moment. A series of nude photos. Not Man Ray, avant-garde-type nudes. Porn nude. Amateur cell-phone snapshots. Ugh, you exhale with the thought, boys will be boys. It's an accepted but repulsive fact that the pornography industry makes about fourteen billion dollars a year, and your husband is a contributor. And didn't one of your friends tell you that porn keeps men from cheating? Silver lining? But then something catches your eye. Even though the photos are focused on the honeypot, there are hands wrapped around the ankles. And on one of the ankles is a tiny rose tattoo. Bingo!

You try therapy, going away to Key West for the weekend, but nothing can bandage the damage that has been done. Your lovemaking is tiresome and bumbling; every time his cell phone rings you worry, is it her? Even your favorite conch-shell salad just tastes like salty mush. There's the infidelity (which is bad enough), but it wasn't off location, outside the sacredness of the family cocoon, it was an invasion of the whole spirit of the house. And you can never erase the images of Sofia's (perfectly manicured) hoo-ha from your mind. Eventually and inevitably, you separate.

Thanks to social media and a Facebook page sent to you by a "concerned" acquaintance, you discover that your ex and Sofia have moved into an all-white, modern condo with one of those Miele espresso makers built into the wall. And adopted a terrier mix they named Fred Flintstone. It may last, it may not. Sofia has cost you your marriage and your home. The only thing you have is your baby. The reason Sofia invaded your world in the first place. And if they end up in a long-lasting relationship, Sofia will become another parent in your child's life. She will have a vote on whether your child will spend Thanksgiving with you or her. Co-opt the college tours, help decorate the new apartment, wrest control over the plans of the wedding . . . she is a terrorist who has taken your life hostage! And a constant reminder that she's just superior in every way.

I'm not saying this will definitely happen if you hire a breathtaking caregiver . . . but a gambler would put a stack of chips on it. I'll never really know because I hired a sixty-year-old woman who bore an uncanny resemblance to Wallace Shawn with no teeth. There's an old real estate saying that applies here: "You always want to be the most attractive house on the block."

CHAPTER 12

THERE ONCE WAS A MAN WHO FLEW TO NANTUCKET

When I give talks, some people seem to mistake me for Dr. Ruth and ask if I really think men and women are that different. Are you kidding me? Aside from the fact that one gender has to haul a couple of testicles around, let's start with the glaringly obvious: If you put a man in a cage for a week and a woman in a separate cage for a week and filmed both, the results would be: her cage—a designer showcase on HGTV; and his—a stomach-churning den from *The Silence of the Lambs*.

Look, I can state the even more obvious: just look at a toilet bowl or hang out in a prison yard. But even putting hygiene and sexual deviancy to the side, I find men's average behavior incomprehensible.

———

We have friends who celebrate every Fourth of July in Nantucket. And when I say celebrate, I'm talking a tribal worship of everything red, white, and blue: face paint, flags, striped clothing, sparklers, and blue food. Nantucket becomes a vomitorium of Americana. And the most fun the Fourth of July could ever possibly be. So when they invited us to join the festivities one summer, I ecstatically bought American-flag bikinis, bandannas, and nail polish. My decision was based on my newfound outlook of embracing life after hitting the middle-age benchmark. I would say yes to things even if they were out of my comfort zone. Yes to fun! And yes, always yes, to lobster rolls!

My husband, older daughter, and I were set to fly on a tiny plane from White Plains, New York, to Nantucket. When we got to Westchester County Airport with our monogrammed tote bags and Stan Smith Adidas, we were told there was "weather" and we had to wait. Indefinitely. So my husband got busy answering the hundreds of emails he had amassed during the drive to the airport, and my daughter discovered there was free Sprite.

I stared out the window and tried to figure out what

"there's weather" meant exactly. I'm not afraid of flying. The idea of being spilled out of the air doesn't worry me, so long as I don't land in water. Where there is water, there are sharks. Man- and woman-eating sharks. If given the choice, I would rather make a resounding splat onto a desert highway to be pecked apart by vultures.

Finally, hours later, we boarded what resembled a toy airplane (I mean this vessel was so minuscule, it's what a 747 eats for a snack) with about eight other strangers. My husband sat up front and we sat toward the back. They said it was a weight issue. I refused to take it personally.

I did notice a particularly dark and ominous sky. But I chalked it up to the aforementioned weather leaving the area. Even though it never actually hit the area. And up into the air we sailed. On a two-propeller plane into the oppressive horizon.

We were about ten minutes into the flight when a bolt of lightning cracked against the sky and lit up the plane like a Miami nightclub strobe. I felt my pancreas leap into my throat, closely followed by the rest of my internal organs. Everyone on the plane let out unedited screams. And the vessel plunged sixty feet before gaining its course again. Don't accuse me of exaggerating—yes, I realize it could have been six feet, but it *felt* like sixty. And I started to smell that pungent stink under my arms—the stench of adrenaline and hormones and fear. The odor one gets before public speaking.

I can count my near-death experiences on one hand. I'm not a thrill seeker. 1) I did hitchhike on the Mass Turnpike in my nightgown, got picked up by a drunk serial killer, and crawled out of the car after it flipped on a bridge. 2) I had an allergic reaction to smallpox. Yes, the horrible disease Pocahontas died from. I didn't die from it (obvi) but spent a summer immersed in Epsom salt baths. 3) There was that break-in in Los Angeles (my mother thinks I dreamt it, but there was a grizzly man in my bedroom—I'm not sure if he meant to harm me or use the bathroom, but he was definitely there!). And then this plane ride.

There was a shockingly loud clap of thunder; the plane seemed to stop moving. It was surreal, like being on a movie set in mock plane seats with a group of production assistants pushing us back and forth, one with a giant fan and another using wooden spoons and copper pots to create the thunder.

It's a hypnagogic feeling to actually contemplate one's demise. I assumed mine would be via a handful of pills and pastries in London's Claridge's hotel. My life didn't flash before my eyes, which I took as a positive sign. But I had a devastating thought about my younger daughter being the only survivor, and who would raise her? Not my mother, my daughter couldn't survive on boiled eggs and PBS. My sisters would fight over her and would choke at the price of her sleepaway camp in New Hampshire. And my girlfriends, well, knowing them, they'd favor their own children, and I'd be damned if my baby was going to clean their chimney and miss out on the ball!

I looked over at my elder daughter. She was sitting upright and frozen. (At least part of that could be chalked up to the fact that she has scoliosis and wears a brace.) We grabbed each other's hands and squeezed hard. I racked my brain, trying to remember if her brace would float or not. How would I unstrap the brace when we were in the choppy water. . . . THE WATER! It's not the thought of drowning that brings on hyperventilation, but (again) SHARKS! And don't try to argue that there are no great white sharks in Massachusetts, because that is where they shot *Jaws*. Not to mention the fact that there have been more than a hundred sightings of great whites off Chatham in the past two years. And they are hungry because their usual feeding patterns have been disrupted. My ass is so meaty and plump right now, I would no doubt be the all-you-can-eat buffet.

BAM! The airplane bounced again, knocking my head against the ceiling. Again, the whole group screamed in unison. A teenager in the seat in front of me burst into tears. I reached my arm over her left shoulder and patted her. She grabbed my hand. I was now stretched between my daughter and the teenager, desperately clutching their sweaty palms. It was silent but for the staccato breaths of panic.

"It's okay," I kept whispering to them. Until another crack of blinding lightning and thunder split open the sky.

"SHIT, WE'RE GOING TO DIE!" It just came out. I had lost control. I couldn't pretend anymore. I was shark bait.

In my spiraling panic, it occurred to me that my significant other, father of my children, and life partner was also starring in the nightmare. He hadn't turned around once. He hadn't asked if we were okay. He showed no concern. Oh God, he must have had a heart attack! Was he dead? Was it possible to distract the sharks with his body?

I unclipped my seat belt and stood up to get a better view. If he was in a state of shock I would need to tend to him. And if he was dead, well, I would have to work out, get Botox, and cut my hair because I'd be out in the dating pool again. Perhaps he was weeping to himself and needed to hear the sound of my voice. I took two steps toward him, trying to steady myself as the floor buckled underneath me like the bouncy castle at a street fair.

And then I saw: HE WAS MEDITATING!

Was he fucking kidding me? We were on the verge of plunging to our death and he was practicing mindfulness? What happened to professing love, throwing his body over ours in the line of fire and burning metal? I was furious. Oh, did I have a mantra for him. My heart was thumping. I was trembling, thinking of ways to save us all, or at least me and my daughter (and the sweet teenager). After all, he was already journeying toward his greater power. I needed to check all my chakras if I was going to rip the rubber raft out of the hands of the other passengers as we descended.

At this point I did what any mature adult in the situation would do: I threw a pen at the back of his head. He jumped and turned to me with a vexed expression on his face. As if to say, "What? Why are you bothering me?"

I couldn't respond. I was speechless. Save for a few startled yelps brought on by another bout of thunder.

Suddenly, the fog parted and I could just make out the small flickering lights of the Nantucket harbor. We would live! But he would die because I was going to kill him! But the rest of us would live!

I could see the cedar-shingled houses with perfectly manicured privets and the Brant Point lighthouse. I've never been so overjoyed to see land. Pretty land. Pretty land of my forefathers now owned by hedge-funders with flamingo swim trunks and nautical art. I deserved a four-pound lobster dipped in butter and salt. With at least two sides. And dessert, dammit.

The plane landed, the windows still streaked with the pelting rain. In silent single file we departed chain gang–style off the plane. All of us still in shock and worried about a future with much PTSD therapy.

And there was my husband ambling ahead of us checking his iPhone like it was just another day of travel. Dum dee dum, wonder what Trump just tweeted?

My daughter and I spotted our friends waiting at the small, quaint airport gate. Their eyes were wide. They had witnessed the storm. They knew. We ran to them and threw our arms around them and held on for an uncomfortable amount of time. I burst into tears. Mama needed to exhale. The group of women, my girlfriends, all hugged and kissed and wiped away tears. My husband got the luggage. Still culling those emails.

We jumped into a Jeep and drove off toward one of the pristine houses covered in pink roses that had been my saving grace when I was up in the air.

I never discussed the event with my husband. The more quickly one makes peace with gender differences, the less angst and frustration one will suffer in life. And people do process things in different ways. I don't have gender prejudice; I just think a woman wouldn't find herself in a downward dog pose while on a runaway train. Maybe the lesson is not to expect that anyone else will save you. Or maybe the lesson is simply: When there's a lightning storm with torrential rain and thunder . . . DON'T FLY!!!

CHAPTER 13

AH YES, FAMILY VACATION

I was lying on a lounge chair in Page, Arizona, in 110-degree heat. A record breaker. The air felt like a perpetual hair dryer, my lips were chapped, and five minutes after emerging from the pool I was completely bone dry again. Wait, this sounds like I'm complaining. And I'm definitely not, because we were on a family vacation and staying at a luxe-y resort where drinks named Serenity and Holistic Desert Green were offered without charge. I had read about the resort nestled in the mesas, blanketed in lavender light, on a lifestyle website. It had everything from hiking to a spa, but what titillated me the most was the fact that you could toast your own s'mores outside your suite overlooking the canyons. I realize I could burn my marshmallows over the stove in Manhattan and smoosh them with some Hershey's chocolate and stale graham crackers, but I like to be in the great outdoors when I inhale chemically enhanced sweets. Maybe because my first s'more was at camp in the Adirondack Mountains. And you never forget your first time.

I had indulged in the roasting-marshmallow ritual every night since we arrived at the resort. In my pj's. Sometimes three or four of the gooey chocolate sandwiches a night. One evening my twelve-year-old daughter looked at me and said matter-of-factly, "Mom, enough with the s'mores . . . have an apple." It stung worse than any rattlesnake bite.

My husband and kids were tubing on Lake Powell all morning. I had very cleverly extricated myself from that particular family activity—something I can rarely do when we are all together on an adventure. We have developed into a very codependent, Eskimo-like squad. We occasionally all sleep together (after a scary movie, in a new place, or when my husband and I are panicking about our mortality), and on vacation we migrate from meal to pool to meal to activity to meal to sleep as a single unit. How I managed to break off from the group being pinballed from one side of the river to another on a steaming hot rubber tire, I hadn't quite figured out. But it was blissful to be perusing the RealReal.com for vintage loafers under a white umbrella drinking a citrusy concoction called a Dream Catcher. . . .

Originally I proposed renting an SUV and driving across country for our June vacation. I had this romantic idea of the kids hitting each other in the backseat, somebody vomiting, and my husband and me bickering about household expenses while the landscape of America flew by us. Let's face it, those are the vacations we all remember. We once took our children to Positano, Italy, and I'm sure they don't remember the stunning villas, the antiquated wooden boats we took to dinner, or the sea urchin pasta we nibbled on overlooking the sunset on Capri. No, they will remember the pasta with butter and cheese. And the fact that we let them watch *Bridesmaids* on the airplane back.

The vague mental film clips of the vacations from my youth consist of my fainting after witnessing a lion disembowel a gazelle's insides in Nairobi, the onslaught of thunderous rain in London, and dysentery in Cuernavaca, Mexico. But my warmest and most lucid memory is being lined up in the back of a Pontiac station wagon with pillows and blankets, squeezed between my siblings, as my mother drove us to Cape Cod through the night. I remember the industrial smells, the phone lines whizzing by the windows, the sounds of the tollbooths, and the restroom stops as we scampered into gas stations in our footsy pajamas. I remember because of the excitement I felt in my belly. The feeling that summer had commenced and we

were on our way to another season spent on the beach—
sandy tomato sandwiches, ice cream trucks, lobster races,
sailing, popping tar bubbles on the road, and long afternoons on a shady wooden porch. It's the ketchup-stained
bathing suits and melted Creamsicles that I want to repli-
cate for my own children. The experience of just being and
having the time to smell the roses (or beach plum blossoms
as it were). Things that don't translate on Finsta.

As I sat back with my hair dripping down my shoulders, perusing the resort's lunch menu, I recalled a family
vacation my husband and I took our girls on a few years
ago. One entirely devoid of tranquility. Or really anything
positive.

My mother had been calling one afternoon nonstop. I
knew nobody was dead; when my mother wants an answer
to something, she simply wants it immediately. After she
left a fourth voice mail, I returned her call. Before I could
get out "Hi Mom," she blurted out, "I think we should go
on a big family trip! You guys; Sissy, Angus, and their families, John and Jen and Fiona and Deitmar." These being
my siblings and their significant others. Now, the idea that
a bunch of adults spread across the country could actually
get their acts and calendars together to sync this imaginary
trip was unfathomable. But my mother's will is stronger
than any assumption. "I hear the Galápagos Islands are

incredible! And soon, the public won't be allowed down there anymore! This is really our last chance to see all the indigenous flora and fauna."

She had me at the word "islands." And the fact that ISIS didn't have a strong agenda in the waters of Ecuador. As I was considering her idea, she blurted out, "Of course I'll pay for the whole trip!" We were going to the Galápagos! Wherever the hell that was!

As is typical in our family, members started dropping out as the date grew closer. My little sister was pregnant. My brother had too many commitments governing the small town of Mammoth Lakes. But most surprising, my mother bowed out. The conductor of the whole moving train. She just "wasn't up to it."

This happened once before when I was twenty-one. My mother had curated a show of the three generations of Wyeth family painters (N.C., Andrew, and Jamie) and it was being historically unveiled in Moscow. I am a Russophile, having always been particularly enamored of Russian history. When my mother was pregnant with me she was reading the novel *Nicholas and Alexandra*. And it was in her second trimester that she decided to name me Alexandrà after the sublime czarina. She didn't finish the book until many months after I was born. And when she finally reached the horrific climax, she learned that Alexandra and her whole family were shot, bayoneted, and clubbed to death by the Bolshevik troops. I suppose my infatuation with Russian history is based on my need for redemption.

So when my mother asked me to accompany her on the trip I was touched and excited and raring to beat up some Bolsheviks. The morning I was set to meet her at JFK for the endless flight to Moscow, she called to say she had come down with the flu. I'll never know if she was truly sick or just exhausted by all the preparation. But I was suddenly flying to Moscow solo. And she's the one who always carried the sleeping pills. I remember standing alone in the security line with a gigantic North Face puffer coat and *The Romanovs* under my arm and thinking, "What the hell am I doing?"

The trip was a life-changing, extraordinary adventure filled with beluga, vodka, a dalliance with a Bolshevik documentarian, and some black market drawings I smuggled home in my suitcase. If my mother had accompanied me, it certainly would have been a different experience—and one where I probably wouldn't have woken up in a hotel room surrounded by a group of gaping Pakistani businessmen.

The Galápagos trip was now me, my husband and kids, and my sister Sissy's family. I considered a switch to Bermuda. The Galápagos struck me as a place that not only needed to be studied and researched ahead of time, but which also involved a certain amount of work during the stay (maps, binoculars, vegetation guides). Bermuda was a beach, a book, some rum, and, at worse, a dented moped.

But while there was plenty of time for me to be lazy (sorry, introspective), I had children—children who needed to see the world and develop into cultivated and erudite adults. They had to earn their rum-soaked beach. It was their turn to appreciate and experience mind-expanding adventures, whether they wanted to or not. We once made them hike up to the Acropolis in sweltering heat; another time they had to ice-pick their way through a fjord in Iceland. These expeditions paled in comparison to the traumatic trek they were about to embark on.

First stop, Quito, Ecuador. Not a spring break destination, but balmy nonetheless. We spent a night in the Hilton there before the family adventure company my mother had randomly googled sent us on a three-day voyage deep into the hills. I believe these tourism travel companies get double kickback points if they can get the tourists into the regions of a country people don't usually venture to. You know, spread the money around. Imagine you're a foreign family coming to visit Philadelphia and they sideline you to Scranton, Pennsylvania, for a few days.

This is when I realized our trip might be veering off the *Eat Pray Love* fantasy and into more of the *Year of Living Dangerously* nightmare. We boarded a rusty bus that rattled for four hours through rocky terrain bordering a steep plummet into bottomless canyons. The ancient, rickety vehicle would have been impounded in the States. Naturally there was a deluge of rain and from the window it looked like a film noir that opens on the hills of Transylvania as the camera pans to Dracula's ominous lair. My teenage nephew started vomiting in harmony with my eleven-year-old daughter's wails. "Get me out of here," she screamed over and over. There's a bizarre sense of resonance when a child vocalizes (loudly) the exact thoughts in your own head.

We finally reached a ramshackle town in the middle of the night. Practically sleepwalking, we checked into our hotel and collapsed. Well, "hotel" is a bit of a stretch, let's call it a flophouse. My husband and I were confined to a miniature, rustic room (not rustic like a Montana lodge, rustic like a prison from the old west). WITH NO WINDOWS. Now, call me spoiled, but when I'm paying money to stay anywhere, I expect two things: a toilet and a window. I think that makes me human, not a princess.

There wasn't much to do in this town, which appeared to be deserted save for gangs of skeletal dogs and a brothel. The only activity we encountered when we drove around that morning was a communal pig roast. Pigs and guinea pigs. As we once owned two life partner guinea pigs, Archie and Lenny, we decided to take a pass. My daughters were traumatized enough. Suddenly the brothel seemed like the better activity for the afternoon.

In those few days in (I forget the name of the town, but let's call it Hogmeat) Hogmeat, we watched all the DVDs we brought with us. Some movies twice. And finally it was time to leave Hogmeat for the Galápagos. Don't think we didn't have to repeat the same treacherous, winding, near-death bus ride back to Quito. And yes, it rained again. This time we were joined by some chickens, which proved a nice distraction from the slippery tires, the vomiting, and the blood-curdling screaming.

We all kept optimistic, sustained by the dangling carrot of the image of pristine islands popping out of the turquoise sea. We didn't even mind it when we were packed into a tour bus without air-conditioning alongside sixty Japanese tourists who didn't speak English and took rapid-speed photos of their seat cushions. We sighed a huge relief when the bus finally braked in front of a dock. A dock coated in bird shit.

We huddled like refugees in matching tattered red life preservers on the dock awaiting guidance. In the water were scattered a few boats. A shiny, lacquered white yacht that should have been named Beyoncé, a *Love Boat* cruise line with all the bells and whistles and I assume a Lido deck, and a rusty tanker that looked like the vessel from the movie *Captain Phillips*. It took about two hours for our group to be assigned to a dinghy covered in clay dust and heading toward our home for the next six days.

Our bow pointed directly toward Beyoncé. I could see white leather chaise longues and what looked like an outdoor pool bar. Something Daniel Craig would climb onto in tight swimming trunks and strangle some bad guys before downing the rest of his martini. I decided I would sunbathe first and then order a virgin mojito. I was going to wait to have my cranial massage on the second day. But suddenly our FEMA dinghy took a choppy turn to the left and we were scraping the rusted metal side of the *Captain Phillips* boat. The Japanese tourists pulled out their state-of-the-art Nikon telephoto zoom lenses and started snapping away. We stopped; maybe we were dropping off some passengers? Passengers who had just joined the navy?

Up the metal stairs with rope safety handles we went. Our (now sopping wet) luggage was flung into a colossal heap on the top deck. We rummaged through it like old ladies at an Irish linen clearance sale, desperately trying to locate our duffels. At one point I decided I'd take one of the bags on top and pray the owner's clothes fit. It's moments like that that I wish I were one of those anal travelers who tie a pretty fuchsia ribbon on the handle of their bag or use a kitten luggage tag for instant identification. My husband has a worn black Tumi carry-on, the same one everyone in the entire world owns. It is the one bag we can never find. On every single vacation we take.

Finally, the luggage was unearthed and we set off on the nauseating journey to find our rooms. Let's not call them rooms; they were bunkers. Most of the passengers ascended, yet we descended, belowdecks . . . BELOW SEA LEVEL! I did not book passage on a submarine. Let me be very clear here—we are a family of anxious claustrophobes who mainline Lexapro; you cannot put us where we cannot see land, light, or some form of oxygen. If I was playing the game "Would you rather" and my choices were sleep in a hazardous cruiser below sea level or lick the toilet seat of a Porta-Potty at a Black Sabbath concert, which do you think I'd choose? You are correct. (Assuming I can bring a can of Febreze, some penicillin, and a mint.)

When my husband and I kicked open the door to room 239, we were met by a fetid stench. Our toilet had overflowed an hour before we embarked. The refuse squished beneath my sneakers. I couldn't open a window because . . . we were underwater.

Our daughters had the bunker next to us, 238. A minute after they dropped their Disney bags, headphones, and bag of gummy bears on the cots, they banged on our door. "We want to go home!" they commanded over and over, an endless loop of wailing. My husband regurgitated one of his greatest lecture hits about being grateful, not being spoiled, and enjoying the moment. I completely agree with him. Most of the time. But when our children were submerged below sea level in a dilapidated tanker with floating shit circling them, the word "spoiled" was not one that sprung to mind. I felt, as Sally Field had in *Not Without My Daughter*, that I needed to find a way to lead my children to safety. And by safety I meant call an Uber.

I pulled out my cell phone and decided to google helicopters in the Galápagos. I figured we could fly to Miami, rent a car, and make our way up the East Coast back to New York. If we only did drive-through McDonald's and switched off driving, we could make it in three days. I got excited. I love Big Macs.

"No cell!"

My husband's head shot up the way our dog's does when you say the word "park."

"What?" he gasped.

"I have no bars. It says no service."

He slipped his feet into his urine-drenched loafers and stormed upstairs. I don't know who he thought he was going to complain to. There was no concierge or Julie McCoy, or even anyone who smiled. And I assumed the captain had his hands full (probably of scotch). My daughters and I scurried up behind him. My husband doesn't get angry very often, but when he does, it's as exciting as it is horrifying—the human equivalent of yellow police tape around a murder scene.

The woman he finally wrangled (I don't even know if she actually worked for the cruise line) barely spoke English, and my husband may be worldly, but Spanish is not in his repertoire. He settled for countering every one of her "No WiFi"s with an "I need it for work." And then the telltale sign appeared—the protruding vein above his temple. All three of us clocked the thermonuclear bomb pulsing on the side of his head. But you can't will cellular connection. And this was my husband's kryptonite. He deflated and took to his soiled cot. Every night he snuck up to the stern of the boat and raised his phone to the sky, Lion King style, hoping for a sign of life. Even from a distant galaxy far far away.

Eating my feelings was not an option. Or eating anything, for that matter. The boat rocked back and forth in such a manner that you were constantly grabbing your silverware so it wouldn't slide off the table. The bottom line was that we were queasy the whole time. It was morning sickness that lasted all day and night without the reward of a baby at the end of it. Instead, a swine's head encased in red gelatin was our dinner reward that night. Now, I can barely get my children to eat anything other than mac and cheese. And their first venture outside their comfort zone was not going to be Pippa the pig's severed head. Thank God for PowerBars.

We had imagined that during the day we would be hiking through uncharted beachfront, swimming with penguins, and discovering subspecies only seen in rare *Harvard Science Review* publications. Nope. We were allowed on shore for two hours a day. We would walk a bit on the gravelly beach and if we were unfortunate enough to miss the sea lions, well, that was just our own bad luck. I've been closer to a sea lion at the Central Park Zoo four blocks from our home.

One afternoon we were granted an hour-long walk on one of the islands fertile with brambles and indigenous

weeds. We had a guide named Louis, a strapping Ecua-
dorian man in his late twenties who would be found on
New Year's Eve two days later, drunk and singing karaoke
to "Borderline" by Madonna. The captain was also very
inebriated that night, which is always a good sign. I had my
eye on the rubber dinghy the whole night; if we did hit an
iceberg (not likely by the Equator), we were going to be the
first family to jump in and paddle to Panama.

Louis pointed out certain trees and a local bird called
the blue-footed Booby. Always made us giggle. As we were
rounding a bend on the dirt path, I spotted a cigarette butt.

"Oh my God! There's a cigarette? How is there a cigarette in the Galápagos? It's so pristine and untouched?"

Louis rolled his eyes. "Sometimes the Russians come
down here with their prostitutes and cocaine and they leave
their trash. It's very illegal. I once found an empty caviar can
in the water."

I love caviar. And I was so hungry.

"Are there any Russians here now?"

Louis shook his head. And dinner that night was pig
face again.

As each day sluggishly went by, my husband's beard
grew longer and his will to live diminished. He would have
beaten out Tom Hanks for the lead in *Cast Away*, I kid
you not. The rocking back and forth that set in on day six
did concern me. Wasn't that what people did when all the
voices in their head were talking at once?

We finally docked at a sketchy fishing town on the coast of Ecuador to await the bus that would take us to the airport and, consequently, freedom, cheeseburgers, and Netflix. We ran off the boat like we were trying to catch the last chopper out of Saigon.

The plane ride home felt like the vacation we were all hoping for. There were peanuts, a movie, and a toilet that actually flushed.

My younger daughter turned to me during the flight and asked, "What do we tell Grandma?"

This was a daunting question. It would be cruel to regale my mother with the litany of the trip's nightmarish experiences, particularly as it had been her idea. And she paid for it.

My daughter's eyes lit up. "I'll just tell her it was a trip we will never forget!"

She got that right.

CHAPTER 14

GOSSIP GIRL

When someone says something unsavory about you, I have found that the confrontational approach rarely works to anyone's satisfaction. Your friend is defensive; you are vulnerable and will probably receive only a mishmash of the truth, which will leave you as frustrated as you were before you decided to talk to this friend in the first place. But I know the feeling! You lose trust, you feel hurt, and you downgrade her birthday gift for years to come.

I am always suspicious of the "heard it from someone who told someone . . ." grapevine. To me it's equivalent to a journalist citing "White House sources." Who are these sources? When has the game of telephone not concluded in a ridiculously scrambled version of the original message? You start with whispering "French fries are my favorite food," and by the time it's repeated back to you it's "Mandela is a flatulent fool." Not the same. Try playing it sometime—just once or twice—it's just as absurd as your naked Twister parties!

———

The real culprit is the nasty, evil-tongued gossip. The words themselves become possessed and the more they are spread, the more demonic they become. Gossip, to me, is more complicated to understand than nuclear codes. The evolutionary theory holds that gossip was used as a tool to bond a group. And as humans multiplied, so did their need for a sense of community, and gossip played a pivotal role in that. Of course, it was mostly practiced among women, and later they were burned at the stake or dunked into a barrel of freezing water, but they did use idle talk to socialize their hamlet. In the sixteenth century the British used to punish the gossipers (or scolds) by forcing them to wear a menacing iron birdcage over their heads. Not helpful if you're gunning for homecoming queen. Imagine a mean girl with blond hair extensions and too much lip gloss walking the high school corridors wearing a metal cage over her head? As punishment, not to straighten a vertebrae.

But today "social bonding" has veered completely out of control—mainly because social media enables gossip to be passed around more quickly than an STD during fleet week. And there's the added perk of potential anonymity.

I had always confused gossip with knowledge. You see, I grew up in Washington, D.C., where gossip was currency in political circles. Gossip could lead to sources that could lead to impeachments, firings, and wars. Well, maybe not wars, but catastrophic events like not being invited to the White House Correspondents' dinner. I would pass the peanuts in my nightgown at my parents' dinner parties and overhear snippets of gossip—"Well, if she keeps screwing that fat Republican, that husband of hers will not be so democratic with the alimony" or "You know, he's a drug addict, so even if he did vote to reauthorize the federal aviation association, he's not going to remember it." And so to me, that's what you did—trade information. Gossip was a way to separate the good apples from the bad. The bruised ones (adulterers, perverts, misbehavers) you knew to toss out. Even if it was just based on rumor. And if you felt the need to chip away at an opponent, you gossiped. "Words have no wings but they fly a thousand miles."

In its elementary form, yes, gossip is lowbrow and wretched and when venomous it can be calamitous for the person being talked about. We have all succumbed to dishing dirt—it's difficult to resist. In the moment you feel such a connection with your coconspirator. It's like sharing a Charleston Chew. You take a bite and munch, then they take a bite and munch . . . soon you're offering other people a piece to chew on! Your adrenaline kicks in when someone tells you something juicy; you can literally feel your heart rate accelerate and you have a burning desire to tell the next person who walks by. "Hey, taxi driver! Open the doors, I've got a story for you. . . . You know that mom who volunteers at the library and walks funny?" In the heat of the moment it's difficult to stop and consider the ramifications. Or to remind yourself that whoever is gossiping *with* you, will gossip *about* you. Or to get really heavy, in Islam they equate gossip with eating the flesh of one's own brother.

I had heard from friends of friends (already a red flag) that a friend of mine was in trouble. Landy was someone who enjoyed a cocktail here, a Klonopin there. The word was that she had gone off the rails and lost control in a spiral of what looked an awful lot like addiction. I knew Landy had an exuberant streak and was pretty much up for anything—spontaneously driving to New England at three in the morning to see the fall foliage or dyeing the tips of her hair a periwinkle blue (she's a grown woman). She was single and childless and a frequent Uber abuser when intoxicated. And by abuser I don't mean she wasn't nice to the drivers, I mean when she was drunk she would take other people's Ubers. Someone told me that once she passed out in the back of the car and woke up in the driver's studio in Queens. He was making ramen noodles as she grabbed her things, leaving behind her bra and one sock. That turned out to be a made-up story.

I was worried about Landy and I took it upon myself to be proactive. I called people—acquaintances, her friends, my friends. I expressed concern and repeated the alarming stories I had heard. There was no malice involved; I was gathering evidence before formulating a plan.

I assumed my conversations about Landy were confidential. Ha ha ha ha, no conversation is ever confidential. (Even with shrinks. I remember once in a session mentioning a friend by name and the therapist saying, "Oh God, don't be friends with her, she's the devil." I'm pretty sure the American Psychoanalytic Association would not find that on brand.) Unfortunately, some people spread the stories, changed the facts to make them more salacious. And others called Landy and told her I was spreading sordid lies—as the kids say, talk'n shit about her.

My first reaction was that of hurt and a sense of betrayal. How dare those people go to Landy when I was acting out of concern and they were interested only in character assassination? But who the hell did I think I was, discussing someone's private life like it was the latest episode of *Dynasty*? And why didn't I just go to Landy first?

I was hardly the victim in this scenario. By the time my words of concern made their way to Landy, they had morphed from "Guys, I think Landy may need help" into

"Landy is a drug addict and got pregnant by her dealer." People found it too delicious not to pepper and season the information.

Landy was devastated. Her reputation had been destroyed and a new unseemly one created in its place. And my hands were dirty. Even if I justified it as genuine distress about her drinking, I had created a "story," a story with momentum. I'm sure if someone told me the stories that have circulated about me, I would never get out of bed.

Along with profusely apologizing to Landy, I went on a gossip cleanse. Which is harder to quit than sugar. Without gossip, I'd be a dullard at dinner parties, I was sure. I'd lose my beguiling, bewitching edge. I would have nothing interesting to say.

My first test was at an intimate dinner with close friends. Now let me state right now: My husband does not gossip. Never has. He will discuss people, just not in a dishy way. So the good news was it wasn't like I was a smoker and quit but my partner still smoked.

At the dinner I found myself starting a sentence like "You know I heard . . ." and then would catch myself and trail off, mumbling like an insane person. But when I left that dinner and the ones that followed, I felt a lightness. I now fall asleep without conversations racing in my head. *Should I have not said that? Will they tell? Well, someone told me, it's not like I made it up. Oh God, I shouldn't have said that.* It helped that my husband monitored me like I had Tourette's, with the fear that at any minute I could scream out "Veronica just had a face-lift!" written all over his watchful face.

I am no longer on a cleanse but a gossip diet. It's easy now. To be positive, happy, peppy, and bursting with love! I'm not going to lie; I still peruse a tabloid now and again and I am as concerned about Brad Pitt's weight loss as the next person. But I don't succumb to spilling tea (gossiping, according to a drag queen pal) about people I know. Or don't know. And without the gossip portion of any social event, you begin to learn that there are plenty of other subjects just as electrifying and that building people up instead of tearing them down does not make you boring or a dullard. As the saying goes, "If you didn't hear it with your own ears or see it with your own eyes, don't invent it with your small mind and share it with your big mouth."

PART III

HALF-BAKED ADVICE

IF YOU CAN'T BE A GOOD EXAMPLE, THEN YOU'LL
HAVE TO BE A HORRIBLE WARNING.

—CATHERINE AIRD

CHAPTER 15

SO LONG, JOE

A few years ago I was given the opportunity to create my own show. Having spent the majority of my thirty-plus-year acting career in a teeny-weeny trailer separated from the male crew's bathroom by a rolling screen, I finally got to be the boss. I was not only the creator, the star, and the writer, but I got to pick snacks (salt and vinegar chips and Rice Krispie treats) and veto wardrobe (no hooker ware unless they're playing a hooker and no open-toe shoes for men).

I can't tell you how many times in the past I'd had to skulk around on film sets in the most unflattering outfits. On the first day of shooting I would giddily peruse the racks of the costume department. All the expensive, ethereal dresses, sharp tailored suits, Manolo heels . . . and then I would stumble upon my segregated area of anemic colors, burlaps, and polyesters. Oh well, that's what the goofy friend, bitchy fiancée, and other assorted nonthreatening females would wear, right?

There was actually one time, on the film *It's Complicated*, that I got to wear the most beautiful Brunello Cucinelli sweaters and shirts, but they were swiftly retrieved on my last day of shooting. Then again, *It's Complicated*'s budget for a day was my show's budget for a whole season. Needless to say, for my show, I brought my own clothes from home.

Another perk of being the boss was that I got to cast the show and hire the crew. I found it the most uncomfortable part of my new showrunner status. I have been that actor with knocking knees in a small, bare room with a camera on a tripod and a few casting people sitting in foldout chairs, bored. I've been the forty-third actress they'd seen that day. There's no other way to say it: Auditioning is an unnatural and inhumane way to search for talent.

So now it was my time to set the tone for the actors coming in, nervous and fidgety, knowing their rent was riding on that one audition—or proof to their parents they didn't have to move back to Pittsburgh. A lot of the actors tried to overcompensate for their jitters with lame attempts at humor. "Whoa, it's like a firing squad in here," chortle chortle. I cringed inwardly, realizing that I had annoyed countless casting directors by plying the same tedious banter. I used to try to sell myself as the gal who would be super fun to hang out with on set—braiding hair, performing pranks, baking cookies . . . they would cast me based on my convivial persona regardless of how mediocre my reading, right?

I met my friend Joe on an independent film set twenty years ago. He was an aspiring director and got his first break (after a series of short films) directing a feature. Making a film is like going to adult sleepaway camp. It's an insular community where everyone pretends to be someone else and eats three meals a day together for weeks; some even sleep together. Joe was confident, handsome, and never ruffled by the craziness surrounding him. He had an "Oh well, I guess that's that" attitude. If he was hauled into a maximum-security prison, he would roll his eyes at the knife fights and gang initiation rites; he would have them all doing trust exercises and starting a band.

I was immediately drawn to him, as I am with most strong men; it's not a daddy issue, I just prefer them to weak men. We shared our life stories on set, meals off set, and we became instant friends. We also bonded because the other actors and crew members were either bipolar and/or alcoholics. It was a good day when one of them got out a whole sentence without having Joe yell cut, or if they emerged from hair and makeup in under three hours.

Over the years we kept in close touch. He lived in

Chicago, so any time I was passing through I made a point of visiting him. I mean, when Oprah was busy, natch. And based on how often I was fogged or snowed in at O'Hare, that was a lot. We grew to know each other's children, marriages, sexual hang-ups, favorite desserts. The important stuff. There was always a Christmas gift exchange. He thought I was thinner than I was, hence the size 2 sweaters and tops, and I'm sure I didn't nail the pajama patterns or sandalwood aftershave, but it was the sentiment and the annual routine that counted. Plus the fact that I actually got a Christmas gift from someone who was not a relative.

When I suddenly found myself in the position to provide my friends with a boost, I swiftly offered Joe a job on my show. No sending tape, interviews, jumping over hurdles, a gift. He hadn't directed in a long time and I always felt he was such an undiscovered gem. Hollywood is known for the climbers who when they claw to the top, they kick the ladder to the ground so that no one below them can ascend; I wanted to share my good fortune, and I was living in New York, not L.A. I also hired our babysitter, who was a struggling actress, and although she's now making a living as a budding TV ingenue, I am out an indispensable caregiver. Who makes the best gouda/avocado/tomato/lettuce/pickles/mustard/cucumber/balsamic vinegar sandwiches on toasted potato bread in the whole world.

We began shooting in late fall in Manhattan. It was frigid outside, but due to an erratic heating system on our set, stifling inside. I did the opposite of what most sane people would do if they were about to shoot a TV show, like dieting and working out; I drank milkshakes and scarfed down midnight pizza. My anxiety was so out of control, I found myself gnawing on my own arm. But it's not like I make a living as a sex symbol (pause for laughter or broaden your mind and look at me in a different light). I'm relatable, which means mildly fetching. Nobody calls Angelina Jolie relatable. In any case, I would cruise the hallways saying no to certain props, no to paint colors, no to certain set designs, and yes to kettle corn.

On Joe's first day he arrived bursting with chummy embraces for the cast and crew. After a brief coffee he was whisked into a production meeting. He was chock-full of cool camera angles, dolly shots, and lipstick camera ideas. The DP and production crew adored him and I knew we were in capable and potentially award-winning hands. Understandably, Joe was chomping at the bit to do something bold and artsy. As any artist would after a long absence of being able to express. He'd been changing diapers for the last ten years. Joe knew it was a test shooting this episode.

On the third day, the network suits were visiting the set. Meaning, the people who granted us the money to produce my cockamamie idea were observing us like laboratory rats to make sure we scrambled around the maze professionally and under budget. They ate doughnuts and drank coffee and apprehensively nodded at juicers (electricians). It was nerve-racking, stressful, and I chewed my nails to the bone (when there were no more doughnuts). Once we commenced shooting, the suits peered over my shoulder at the monitors like they were scrutinizing the world's first brain transplant. And occasionally offered me helpful hints like, "Can you retake it and make it funnier?"

Joe was beaming, but I could tell beneath his strut there was an undercurrent of unease. It had been a long time since he was behind the camera, a few feet away from a bunch of farting crew members checking their Snapchat. That said, I figured Joe knew what he was doing; he didn't need me to give him any direction.

After a few takes, the suits, my partners, and I realized Joe was giving the actors somewhat bizarre notes. They were playing it like an avant-garde Cocteau play. Very staccato and austere. We cut. In an upbeat way I bounced over to the set.

"Hey Joe!"

"Hey Sweets!"

"Listen, I think you're maybe putting too much depth into this. It's just a comedy! These characters are pretty cookie cutter and the jokes are pretty blatant . . . so just roll the camera and don't make it so difficult on yourself. You'll make it amazing no matter what."

I stepped back behind the monitors, which were no longer filled with chitchat and snacks. It was somber and the suits looked stressed out. Even my partners stared at me like dogs on the last day at a kill shelter.

And action! Again, we were watching some macabre Off-Broadway play. The jokes landed like lines from a Sylvia Plath novel. This was not the show I created! Dear God, this wasn't even a comedy! And that's pretty much all I'm capable of! The suits started mumbling about finding another director and eyeing me like I might have stolen their wallets. Or voted Republican. I was in trouble.

At its core, my marriage is a rocklike partnership. And I trust my husband's judgment more than my own most of the time. Not about road rules or my ideal fighting weight, but the biggies—moral and ethical stuff. He is a church-goer and possesses a sound moral foundation, particularly around the areas I find gray—like what's wrong with murder if he cheated? Or if the cash register's open, doesn't it make the money free? And so I did what I've done a million times before when in need of crisis management. I emailed my husband. And, as he is my spouse, we have a shorthand. In other words, we're beyond diplomacy. My email was simple: "Help. Joe sucks. I'm going to have to fire him." Send. I figured he would reply with the same suggestion I was already arriving at, to talk through the show and get on the same page (or the same book in the same language). Because we were friends, I had mistakenly assumed Joe "got" the show. And assuming makes an ass out of only me.

I found myself wishing that I was back in some shitty trailer next to the crew's men's room reading *InStyle* magazine. When you're the boss every problem is your problem. You can't point the finger at sweet Gary, whose job it is to pass enchiladas around at break. I turned to one of the writers, hoping he had an idea of how to pull us out of the mess. He was finishing an economy-size bag of Swedish Fish. "I'm just a writer." I felt my phone vibrate from my back pocket. Ah, sage words from my husband. He would fill the hole I had dug—with what, I didn't care. I glanced down. A reply from Joe. I HAD ACCIDENTALLY SENT THE EMAIL TO HIM.

My instinct was to hide under a card table in the corner. "Oh my God, oh my God, oh my God," I kept repeating. My mind raced: How could I have done that? How could I have been so stupid? And how could I make it all go away? I needed that zapper from the film *Men in Black* that could erase a person's recent memory. I had never in my life sent an email to the wrong person. I had heard stories—the guy who sent his wife the sexy email instead of his mistress, a friend who replied all to a group of women, one of whom she was bad-mouthing. . . . I threw my phone on the floor like it was covered in blood. Maybe if I destroyed the source, the last five minutes of my life would simply reboot? Then I had the imbecilic idea that if I could find his phone I could delete the message. That wouldn't work, Sherlock, because *HE HAD ALREADY READ IT!*

I took a deep breath. He was my friend. I had to face the storm.

Now, on the spectrum between protecting feelings over the cold truth, my tendency is to protect feelings. If friends ask me if they look too old, too fat, or if their powder room is gaudy, I find it easier to say no. I don't ever want to upset anyone. I'm very nonconfrontational. Unless it involves my children, and then I'll cut you.

I rushed to the set. There was only a key grip lying on the floor listening to Coldplay. I scrambled to find Joe, sticking my head into random opened doors until I found him alone in the editing bay. Door closed. I paused. I had felt this way once before, when I jumped out of a plane into the California desert. At least then I thought there was a chance I might die.

"Hey!"

"Hey," he said lightly.

"Listen, sorry about the email mixup. I was typing so quickly, I meant to say 'Joe, HE the actor, sucks and we may have to fire HIM.'"

"Ahhh, I thought it was strange you would email me that."

A rush of heat overtook my body. A deceitful hot flash.

When I left the editing room, I told myself that my spin doctoring had actually worked. It was illogical and implausible, but I bought that he bought it. Had I really just piloted myself out of a raging shit storm? No matter what, all I wanted was to shield him from hurt feelings and preserve the friendship.

I was still left with the problem of the scenes. Now if I commented on his directing he would know that the email was, in fact, about him. My hands were tied. So I said nothing. I had no choice but to let him continue shooting in the aforementioned bizarre way until we wrapped the episode. And he never let on that there was an issue.

A few weeks later, however, I received an email. As it was a private exchange, I will say only this. He did know I was referring to him. He was hurt and humiliated. And he ended the email with the words "So long."

Those words spun me out for weeks. The quote "The worst thing about being lied to is knowing you weren't worthy of the truth" echoed in an endless loop in my head. Why hadn't I just told him from the start that what he was shooting was striking the wrong tone? He would have changed it and everybody would have been happy! I had completely dropped the reins. I had been unduly concerned about the balance of power, how he would react to me within the hierarchy of the set. Yes, it's challenging to work with friends, but I made it impossible.

The difficult lesson was that in trying to protect his feelings, I chose to lie (a pathetic lie) to preserve his dignity when, in fact, it accomplished the opposite. Always choose the truth. As my mother used to say, "A truth may hurt for a little while, but a lie will hurt forever." Dammit, she was right again.

To this day, he has refused to speak or see me. And

although I empathize with the pain I caused him, I'm sad. Sad that a twenty-five-year friendship perished from one accidental email.

Don't lie—and if you must, always triple-check your emails before hitting send. And listen: If you live in the Chicago area and bump into a director named Joe, tell him I miss him. Very much.

CHAPTER 16

TINY LIFE

I f you never have sex with your partner then you have a huge problem. And this is coming from a girl who hails from a long line of WASPs who choose gin and tonics over carnal delights and probably haven't felt anything from the waist down since the 1880s. You must have sex with your partner. It doesn't have to be done with a light show, a feather boa, and a can of coconut milk. Nobody needs to swing from a leather harness into a vat of dark chocolate. But there is something to the one intimate act that you share exclusively with that person. It defines your relationship as sacred. I'm not preaching from a religious pedestal here, this is basic human optimism. Now, if you have some sort of mutual agreement that allows other arrangements that includes twins, strangers, and your neighbors, I am intrigued to know how that actually works. You must be exhausted.

Let me regale you with a cautionary tale. Sadly, you may have heard similar ones before. I have a friend named Tyne, who lives in Philadelphia. She is a kindhearted, charitable, warm woman who is beloved by everyone who knows her. Tyne had a tumultuous childhood punctuated by a series of divorces due to a bipolar mother resulting from fraud, alcoholism, and infidelity. Consequently, Tyne went to live with her uncle, who was barely present in her life. And she ran away from home when she was sixteen, with a pothead who believed that one day marijuana would be legal and when it was he was going to exploit it and become a billionaire. Silly boy. They lived in a Volkswagen bus in Big Sur for a few years before he fell in love with a local surfer whose father owned the tattoo parlor in town. Tyne ended up in San Francisco waitressing in a coffee bar. (The boy eventually became the billionaire owner of some of the largest medical marijuana companies in the world. But he still has the name "Tyne" inked on his ankle. Next to the one of Jesus catching a wave.)

After getting her heart broken, Tyne vowed she would not re-create her past with her chosen family and future children. She would grab stability and predictability by the wilting balls. And all the practical, undramatic things that accompany them.

On a hot summer evening near the wharf in San Francisco, at a clambake littered with plastic wineglasses and J.Crew madras shorts, Tyne met Leopold. He was a young lawyer working for a reputable firm that specialized in trusts and estates. He was also a gentleman, refreshing her spritzer and introducing her to his friends in a way that was socially adept and also a smidge territorial. Tyne felt safe. And he was handsome, with thick wavy blond hair and light blue eyes.

Their dates were pretty ordinary—a dinner in Chinatown, a movie, and lots of lattes. If their courtship had been billed as a romantic comedy, you would have thrown down your uneaten Twizzlers and demanded your money back. That's if you made it past the first five minutes.

It wasn't a particularly passionate union. The first time she slept over, they got the job done (who knew who was faking), but both were more interested in trying to figure out how to work his TiVo. It became one of those "You know what? This is fine" kind of unions.

After a year, they got engaged. Decorum stated it was time. Not too fast, but not overly protracted. Tyne sighed with relief that she had found a respectable husband. And he was a lawyer! She couldn't wait to pass around carrot sticks and dip on her new Gump's white porcelain with gray trim wedding china. This was payback for her erratic and depressing childhood. She had won.

Soon Leopold was offered a job at a more prestigious

law firm that specialized in tax evasion and shelter. They bought an ivy-covered brick mansion in the historic and affluent Main Line area of western Philadelphia. Leopold complained about the expensive mortgage, which became an obsession and discussion at every soiree. "My wife just had to have it," he would say. This being his sexist salute to giving the woman who bleaches his underwear something to show off about, when really the humble brag was meant to trumpet his own financial worth. Anyone who truly cannot afford something keeps it to himself. Tyne's concerns were what botanical club to join and where to buy the Yves Delorme sheets she had seen in other fancy homes.

Tyne completed her fairy-tale family by having a baby boy. (To be childless on a holiday card is to advertise a wrinkle, an issue, a prick in the bubble.) She pushed her British pram through the park for all to see—she was a mother and her baby was perfectly tucked into a blue cashmere blanket. As she looked up at the cloudless September sky, Tyne finally felt she had it all. The dark shadows of a splintered, bipolar-plagued past were far behind her.

I met Tyne when she was in the full bloom of her new life. Her son, Grayson, was at the most prestigious preschool, and she had committed herself to transporting him to school, horseback, and Mandarin lessons. She joined superfluous clubs that sponsored historical organizations and society galas and trunk shows where she would drink wine and overpay for costume jewelry.

Tyne and I had mutual friends and because Leopold had court cases in New York we met at a Manhattan dinner party and became fast friends. I never really connected to Leopold. I was put off by his blowhard personality and the way he undermined her. Tyne may have learned her mannerisms and etiquette from some outdated Palm Beach magazines, but I was attracted to her vulnerability around the edges. She got the joke. Even the dirty ones. And she was game.

It was eight years later. I could barely make out the words, let alone who was screaming them into my iPhone that afternoon. After a few more wails and some panicked breaths, I realized it was Tyne. "I can't, I can't, I can't," she kept repeating.

Tyne had gotten up at 6:00 A.M., as she always did, to make her son breakfast before he got on the bus to school, something she had done for the past thirteen years. Frozen waffles, watered-down orange juice, and three strawberries. Repeat. That particular morning, Tyne had been suffering from a bout of insomnia. She knew that if she watched *The Fugitive*, she wouldn't be able to sleep, but she loves Harrison Ford. So she poured herself a strong cup of instant coffee.

Grayson made his way to the kitchen, his face intent on his cell phone, his eyes never drifted from the screen glow even as he devoured a bite of waffle drenched in syrup.

"Where's Dad?"

"I don't know. He might have had an early case today."

"He left his computer."

Tyne looked over to the living room and saw Leopold's computer lying on the carpet. How Grayson could even see that in his peripheral vision, she couldn't understand. He grabbed his knapsack and a banana and bid his mother good-bye, never taking his eyes off his own screen. She heard the front door slam and smiled to herself. What a terrific kid she had: smart, handsome, a whiz at physics, and an exemplary lacrosse player. He was like a Kennedy.

Tyne quietly picked up her husband's laptop and placed it on the mahogany dining room table. A table that bore testament to their life as a family through its scratches from Thanksgiving mishaps and steaming pots of bolognese scorching the surface. Leopold works so damn hard, she thought to herself, and decided she was going to buy something butterscotchy for dessert that night. Leopold loved butterscotch.

Before she closed the laptop, she caught a glimpse of something pink and fleshy. She clicked on the image. It was a man. A naked man. Holding his . . . manhood. Above the photo was a message: "Miss you Boo!" in pink script. Tyne froze for at least two minutes. All kinds of wires sparked as her brain tried helplessly to reboot. Mechanically, she sat down on one of the dining room chairs. And did what every woman would do in this situation. She went cyberhunting. And she went deep. Tyne wasn't very tech savvy, but she knew how to hit the history tab.

Leopold had apparently fallen in love with Colin some years back. She couldn't discern exactly where they had met, but based on the different swim trunks Leopold wore in many of the photos (all of which she had given him on birthdays and Christmases) she could piece together a basic timeline. There were files of romantic getaways on boats with their arms looped around each other's waists, sharing bowls of pasta, and clinking glasses in front of what looked like a tropical-getaway sunset. The photos, along with the love notes (some complete with heart emojis), were all concealed under fake case folders. *Griffith v. Stockwell* housed photos from what looked like a country inn. Food photos, fireplace photos, and Colin in a bulky fisherman's sweater gazing into the lens.

Tyne then did the second thing most women would do in her situation: She ransacked her house for evidence. As if the hard drive didn't tell an explicit enough story, she searched for tangible evidence. After all, she was a lawyer's wife.

Hours later, she was shaking and crying at my kitchen table. "I don't understand," she kept repeating.

"I think it's pretty clear, Tyne; your husband is gay."

"But he's not." She looked at me like a toddler who believes in Santa.

"Let me ask you this, how often did you guys have sex?"

"Umm, I don't know, we haven't had sex in about ten years?" CUE THE ALARMS, RED FLASHING LIGHTS, EMERGENCY BOMB SIREN!

Men have sex. And if they're not having it at home, chances are they are having it somewhere else. It's scientific; it's biological; it has been happening for centuries. Tyne was so caught up in the performance of this perfect life, she was content to sacrifice her own sexuality, and ultimately her life, if that would keep the status quo.

"Why? Why didn't you guys have sex?"

"He never wanted to." And she accepted that. Tyne chose a perfect Christmas card over an orgasm.

It doesn't matter that Leopold strayed with a man, another woman, or if he'd chosen a goat. Sex is the barometer of true intimacy. If you are not engaging in a physical relationship, you are basically just living a transactional existence. You are roommates. And you should split the rent, watch Netflix, and cruise eHarmony.com together. But don't kid yourself that a nonsexual union can sustain itself without one of you sticking a hand in another's cookie jar.

I'm thrilled to say that Tyne is now dating the hunky check-in guy at her gym. Who knows where it will lead, but hey—baby steps. The point is, she's never been happier. And she's realized what she's been missing all these years . . . sometimes twice in one day.

CHAPTER 17

AND THEY CALLED IT PUPPY LOVE

I think I had my midlife crisis in my thirties way before I was married, had kids, and was disheartened by my career. I fell into relationships that lasted way past their expiration dates and was cast in one sitcom bomb after another. I'm glad I got it over with early. I would not want to be a ninety-pound chain smoker who refuses to get out of bed now. Well, maybe one hundred pounds wouldn't be so bad. I'm a late bloomer in every other facet of my life—first kiss at sixteen, ability to make mature decisions at forty, and discovery of fitness . . . well, not quite there yet. It's curious my midlife spiral set in so prematurely, but then again, my friend Layla went through menopause at the age of thirty-two, so you just can't predict.

Since I got off the court early I have a prime spectator seat for witnessing the U.S. Open of everyone else going bananas. Cuckoo, barmy, cracked, trippy, bobo, whack . . . At least a large portion of my friends. Some act out the cliches of your typical affair or kiss someone of the same sex (drunk at game night) and some take the less obvious route of seeking vaginal rejuvenation. Now let me just say this—do not touch your vagina with a scalpel or scissors unless there's an honest-to-god medical reason—i.e., there's a thumb sticking out of it or you're transitioning. If it is for purely aesthetic purposes or to reclaim the genitalia of a twenty-year-old, DO NOT (I repeat) cut and paste your bits. Go to therapy for at least a year. And, God forbid, if your partner suggests it . . . ? Well, go to therapy with him for a year. Or better yet, dump him.

My bias against this procedure is not based on firsthand experience; I can't even look at my vagina, let alone give it a spa day. I simply think designer vagina surgery is expensive, risky, and painful. It's good puritan common sense: Shaving off your labia will not make you a happier person. It will just make you walk funny. But who am I to say? You only have onegina.

Another midlife trend I've observed is the impulse to move. It's distracting, it's time-consuming, and it promises the hope of a better life, one with lacquered walls and built-ins. For some it's the joy of renovation that motivates them—and I get that; if I could, I would move every six months. My dream is to be a castle flipper. Take a castle in Ireland or France, revive and refurbish it, and then move on to the next palace. Sadly there isn't much of a market for that. And I can't find solid gold molding at Home Depot. So I just spend afternoons lying on the couch gazing at paint swatches. And wondering what fish to stock my moat with. But I have seen friends zigzag across the country searching for the meaning of life. And a three-bedroom with water views. But what you are moving from cannot be outpaced. And even Chernobyl looked good in the brochure!

———

I did have a mild flirtation with a midlife crisis a couple of years ago. I found myself bolting awake in the middle of the night, plagued by empty-nest nightmares. My twelve- and fourteen-year-old daughters were flapping their wings. What if one of them moved to Kazakhstan? Well, that wasn't realistic—there's no Pinkberry there. But what if neither of them wanted to spoon-feed me applesauce and change my bedpan when I was old . . . er. By law, wasn't the younger daughter required to forfeit her right to marriage and happiness to become a spinster and care for her aging parents? Our adult diapers were not going to change themselves! Wasn't that written somewhere in the Constitution or the American Girl catalog? I nudged my husband, not in the "let's get it on" way but in the "there's a serial killer in the attic go deal with it" way.

"Hey, hey . . . I think we should adopt a baby."

"Okay." He snorted.

I lay back down, calmly narrowing down names for my sweet Syrian refugee cherubs. Yes, I would be (by far) the oldest mother in kindergarten, but I could camouflage myself in ripped jeans, sneakers, and hair extensions. I couldn't decide on two or three babies. My back was shot, so they couldn't be lifted. But babies live on the kitchen floor anyway. I forgot about colic. Yeah, that might be a deal breaker. And teething . . . how was I going to get my eight hours of sleep with my sweet angels screaming at the top of their lungs? With perimenopause I sometimes treated myself to a crumb of Xanax to deal with the insomnia; what if I didn't hear them? Or their screaming got to me and I took too many? The more I ruminated on the idea, the more I realized how unfair it would be to use adorable Lily or baby George to fulfill whatever lingering maternal instincts I possessed and to fill a much larger hole of fear of abandonment. However, with the clarity of a good night's sleep and the vision of creating a light gray elephant–themed nursery, baby George was still not off the table.

So I did what millennials do when they feel dispirited (or depressed, angry, or fill-in-the-blank emotion): I went online. Unlike them, I did not peruse Tinder, Grinder, iHookup, or FriendFinder. I went on Petfinder.com. Far more temptation . . . and with Petfinder, it's not just for one hookup, it's for life!

Sure, I could have gone for the obvious puggle, buggle, suggle, or other man-made, mass-produced cuddly canine. But I've never been a fan of forced breeding. I clicked on a rescued pit bull. Too fit. Like he spent his life in a canine Gold's gym. No matter how many SoulCycle or Pilates classes I could enroll in, he would always have superior muscle mass; I'd look like Betty White walking Arnold Schwarzenegger. My finger swiped through hundreds of dogs. I would pause occasionally to imagine myself with a particular pooch. Would we make a good couple? Could I see us together? Was he breastfed?

And then I found him. And I knew. Like when you see dark chocolate–covered potato chips. You don't need to try them to know they're perfection. My heart almost burst out of my faded pink monkey pajamas. Sure, it was his looks (I'm as superficial as the next gal), but there was something else, something beneath his penetrating gaze. He knew who he was. He was young, about sixteen weeks, but something told me he was an old soul. He had silky, short black hair with a striking white lightning bolt down the center of his face. Those deep, mahogany eyes a girl can get lost in. He would be large, based on the size of his paws, but not massive. Probably not an athlete, but definitely athletic. Maybe not football, but certainly he would chase a tennis ball. I swiped through a few more mutts but couldn't get his face out of my head. As I used to say after the first time I met my husband, like a good melon, you just know!

In life you have to take risks. You listen to your gut, you take the plunge, you throw caution to the wind. You throw a dog a bone.

Cooper arrived on a Sunday afternoon in August. He had a tragic childhood, according to the shelter papers. His mother was a homeless beagle in Arkansas with heartworms that gave birth to a litter of puppies moments before being euthanized. Cooper's brother was killed in the shelter by a gang of dogs. His sister was adopted a few weeks before him. But all this occurred in his infancy, so I figured therapy was unnecessary. And he seemed so happy! This was definitely not going to be a Prozac pet. I saw how much my dad spent medicating his cat, Monty. That cat was a serial rapist but was so doped up he just lay catatonic on the rug all day.

When Cooper jumped out of the animal transit truck it was as if he had been released from a week at Bible camp. He couldn't run, lick, pee, or jump fast enough, so it all happened simultaneously. Just once I'd like to witness my kids behave like that when I place dinner on the table.

The first few months I was in a constant state of puppy love. Everything he did was adorable to me. I became one of those people who walked around the yard saying (in a cartoon voice) "Who's a good boy? Huh? Who's a good boy? Who's Mommy's perfect baby from our Lord Jesus Christ?" Yes, he disemboweled a few pieces of furniture and splattered poop Jackson Pollock–style across the hallway carpet, but he never barked loudly or held up his paw to me. And he could read my thoughts. When I put on my sneakers and reached for his leash, it was as if we were communicating telepathically: He knew I was taking him to the park! Oh, the park . . . how many rapturous afternoons we have spent lying in the grass and running up the rocky knoll as if in a flea-collar commercial. One day we were chasing squirrels and we both got peckish, so we bought a couple of hot dogs from a street vendor. And wouldn't you know it, Cooper, always watching out for me, jumped up and devoured my hot dog. He knew I wasn't eating carbs that week.

I think Petco should host a perimenopause adoption day the first Saturday of every month. It would save many women from making ungodly mistakes. And it's more fulfilling than Wellbutrin. Who wouldn't want to be greeted with such exuberance when you walk in the door? Cooper leaps onto the bed the second he hears me brushing my teeth. Granted, so does my husband, but for different reasons. And even though Cooper loves me just the way I am, he encourages me to take him to the park or the beach every day until we're both tuckered out. No trainer could ever motivate me like Cooper. But then again, no trainer ever licked my face.

If I want to be reclusive and watch the USA Network marathon of *Law & Order SVU*, he is content coiling his body around mine with a paw on my thigh. He might not understand the mature content of the show, but he's peaceful knowing we are at rest. And that at the end, Olivia Benson will prevail.

My husband is not a jealous man. There's no reason for him to be. But he has started referring to my pup as "boyfriend." "You with your boyfriend?" Even though my boyfriend is a hound mix that eats other dogs' poop, just the titillation factor of the word is very satisfying. I mean, my husband better keep on his toes, or at any minute Cooper and I could shoplift a large London broil and make haste to Mexico.

You don't want an affair! It's messy, painful, and requires so much extra grooming. And if you are someone who believes self-mutilation is the answer, then I can't help you. But there are doctors in Malibu who probably can. Listen to me—I cannot howl this loud enough—get a dog! If you're allergic or they don't allow dogs in your building, get a cat or a chinchilla or a damn betta fish (although with a fish I can't promise you'll get that unconditional love; they don't really cuddle). One last piece of advice: Don't get suckered into bunnies (even on Easter) because they do multiply faster than the national debt—nobody can handle that much unconditional love.

AND THEY CALLED IT PUPPY LOVE

GIVE A MAN ONE RABBIT, AND HE WILL EAT FOR A
DAY; GIVE A MAN TWO RABBITS, AND HE WILL FEED
HIS FAMILY AND HIS NEIGHBORS AND RETURN YOU
64,768 RABBITS IN CHANGE.
—ANONYMOUS

CHAPTER 18

LET THEM GO

went to an organic summer camp called Mountain Peaks Camp, in the Adirondacks, when I was nine years old. Let me be more precise: I was shipped off, as most of my friends and siblings were, for an enriching two-month retreat that served the dual purpose of giving my parents a break from not having to hear "I'm bored" all summer, and me some fresh air and a sabbatical from an obsession with *Charlie's Angels*. Looking back, all the parents must have been elated to have us out of their hair, what with all the key parties and marijuana Crock-Pot mixers going on. As our parents were experimenting with weed and one another, we were planting rhubarb and mucking out horse stalls.

On the first day, the hills were alive with sounds of screaming as my trunk was brought to my tent. A tent in a forest of mosquitoes and no air-conditioning. I was a somewhat needy child who had a difficult time expressing myself (I held on to the bumper of our Volvo for two hours). This was years before email and texting, so all communication was restricted to handwritten letters. It's hard to fathom now that a heartfelt missive on Snoopy stationery concerning a horrible bout of homesickness wouldn't elicit a reply for ten days. I even wrote SOS with pinecones on the craggy beach. The first week my only friend was an overweight pony called Popcorn.

And here's the most devastating part—we weren't allowed sugar. I know. Criminal. Once in a while we got strawberry-rhubarb pie sweetened with raw maple sugar. Some parents tried to hide candy in thermoses, cut tennis balls, and the sleeves of sweatshirts, but it was always confiscated. And probably inhaled in the counselors' private quarters that same night. I remember we once snuck into our counselor Julie's tent looking for candy and found what we thought was a sink stopper. We borrowed it to play Frisbee and eventually lost it somewhere out by the lake. Turns out it was her diaphragm. Julie must have had a very frustrating summer.

We spent an extraordinary amount of time weeding the garden, which took up about an acre of the camp property. When you are detoxing from potato chips, Twinkies, and Marshmallow Fluff, raw fennel stalks are delicious. So when you were lucky enough to stumble upon a raspberry bush? It was like being in a 7-Eleven with no supervision and a hundred-dollar bill. When we had day trips to pick blueberries, I would inhale them until I choked and had purple teeth. And don't get me started on the peanut butter and horsefly sandwiches we created for afternoon snacks!

When you were an older camper, you were allowed to go on overnight camping trips. Sometimes they would last as long as four or five days. Without a toilet. Not recommended for kids with anxiety. You saw nothing but trees for hours, had no idea where you were most of the time, and obsessed over how you would be killed by the cannibal madman who lived in a cave. We would scale the peak of Mount Marcy wearing twenty-pound backpacks filled with dented pots, cans of Sterno, and water bottles. It was like an army video for teens. Dinner was goulash and crackers heated over a fire. Occasionally they would mix it up and we'd have hot dogs and beans (which I still love, but my husband won't eat). After the gassy cuisine we would spread out our sleeping bags in a sweltering tent and try to position ourselves so that we wouldn't be lying on a knobby tree root. If you did happen to lie on a knobby tree root, you would walk like a pregnant woman the next day, belly out, clutching your lower back.

I had a best friend at Mountain Peaks Camp. Her name was Anne. Anne was from Westchester, wore braces, and had a boy's haircut. She was emotionally cushioned by the fact that she had an older brother and a younger one at the camp. But that didn't stop her from waking me up the first night, as I was sniveling into my pillow, and telling me a made-up story about how she had a sister who died. I think she did it to distract me. God, I hope so.

Anne was with me on one of these Navy SEAL overnights. After two days our hiking boots were mangled, we had moss and mud permanently embedded on the backs of our ankles, and we smelled like Off! Deep Woods insect repellent spray. When we walked the last few steps from the trail onto the camp property, it felt like we were coming back from the first lunar walk. Everyone greeted us with hugs and questions about what we saw, what we did, who had developed a crush on who. You know, post-being-in-space stuff. And then we were allowed to shower. Not a long hot shower, a warm trickle with biodegradable soap and some antifungus slippers. It felt blissful washing the dead, bloodied insects off my legs and throwing away my pee-pee rag. (That is a washcloth used every time you urinate so as not to trash the environment with paper. It was tied to the back of our packs. Nothing brings all the boys to the yard like a waving rag of waste matter!)

A week after that trip, Anne developed a high temperature and was taken to the infirmary. Nobody actually went to the infirmary. All of the counselors had calamine lotion and Band-Aids, so unless you needed open-heart surgery, the infirmary was just a strange wooden cabin at the edge of camp with a red cross painted on the door.

A few days went by before I begged to visit Anne. At that age your best friend was your life. You shared secrets, handshakes, and even blood. Tell me you never pricked your finger until it bled and pressed it together with your friend's? Well, you're never too old.

When I tiptoed into Anne's room, she was rolling around and sweaty. She was delirious. And needed an exorcism. It turned out she had contracted typhoid fever from the stream water. A day later she was sent home. One of the most devastating moments in my life.

The camp overlooked Craggy Cliff Lake, which, if you were nine years old, seemed like the Atlantic Ocean. Three times a week we had to swim a half mile. Now, I couldn't swim a half mile today if you promised me a Tesla and Ryan Gosling covered in dark chocolate. But back then I had no choice. It could be hailing and we would still have to combat the choppy waves while a counselor covered in a tarp rowed alongside us. I was the only kid who shivered, turned a delicate shade of blue, and held on to the rowboat like I had just been rescued at sea. For me, those swims were the most physically challenging tasks to date. Which trumpets my physical weakness, I get that, but I would've rather run the Boston Marathon.

Even the arts and crafts, which one would imagine consisted of a few beads and a string, was equivalent to a University of California, Berkeley, graduate arts program. I loomed blankets, place mats, and pot holders. I threw so much clay that I brought home enough plates and bowls for a small banquet. And the wood shop? I whittled two canoe paddles. I may not use them very often, but if I were ever the sole survivor in a plane crash and lost in the wilderness, I would be able to cut down a substantial pine tree and carve out a sailboat. Now, I would be in the forest so a boat would do me no good, but I would take comfort in knowing that I'm skilled! And I could also use my cell phone to get help.

At camp they encouraged us to play a game that would be banned today. It was called Mumbly Peg. Each child was given a Swiss Army knife the first day of camp. They now have metal detectors at schools to prevent things like that, but at camp they were given out like sunscreen. And we were taught various knife games and tricks. Most of them involved flipping the knife and having it land centimeters from our fingers. We would sit out on the sprawling, freshly mown meadow and fling knives at one another. I imagine they don't support this sport anymore. It was then the 1970s and I believe the Mumbly Peg counselor (three-finger Pete) is probably dead by now.

As much as I complained, almost cut my arm off with a saw, and ate porridge that tasted like melted glue, I returned to the camp year after year until I aged out. It was a sad day for me in the backseat of our car cruising down the dusty road that led away from the camp knowing I would never be back again. I still dream about it. And Anne is still one of my best friends.

I can compost anything, oil a horse hoof, and make you a macramé belt. Come on, who doesn't love a macramé belt? That can also turn into a plant holder? But, more important, going to camp helped a little city girl with high abandonment and anxiety issues about leaving her comfort zone pull herself up by her hiking boots, straighten her overall straps, and throw herself into a world that would build confidence and form the woman she is today. (You know I'm talking about me, right?)

So give your children flight. . . . It's not easy. You can't FaceTime. But you are giving them experiences they can only have without you. And I say this while my older daughter is calling me from camp hysterically crying and threatening to get herself kicked out.

"Not unless you come down with typhoid!" I always say.

CHAPTER 19

SEX TAPE

I don't care if you are blessed with a Victoria's Secret body (or even if you are an actual Victoria's Secret model) naturally or courtesy of renowned plastic surgeon Dr. Hidalgo. Wear the lingerie, wear the damn wings, jump around in the nude in the privacy of your own room, fine. Just don't send images into the ether, where your grandchildren can inadvertently find them when googling info for your eulogy twenty years from now.

I realize that I risk coming off like a prude here. Every teenager in America has probably sent a sexy selfie by now. And in the digital age of pornographic images selling everything from cheeseburgers to cat litter, why not? Even celebrities find it paramount to expose their asses as much as possible. There is some perverse pleasure in having their bodies graded like an episode of *So You Think You Can Dance Naked*? And I am not a prig by any stretch of the imagination; I've been nude before. When I was a toddler. I just worry about the overall effect—on women in particular.

You may imagine that I'm only saying these things because I am not a twenty-year-old with a flat stomach and boobs that reside above my belly button. That I studiously avoid catching any glimpse of my naked self in mirrors. And that as I crawl into bed with my husband at night wearing a huge T-shirt and pajama pants, I always offer a downcast "I'm sorry." But even if I had Gigi Hadid's body, I would never be inclined to show the world everything one shares with her gynecologist. (A bikini shot is another thing. I mean, it's Gigi Hadid's body!)

Maybe we're reverting evolutionwise. The clothes are coming off and soon we will be walking on all fours? I wouldn't mind that: no waxing and shaving! You'll need that welcome mat of pubic hair to stay warm.

And my prohibition extends to the dreaded "dick pics" as well. Now, I've been married for sixteen years, so perhaps I'm not the target audience, but if a man sent me a photo of his penis and we barely knew each other? I would immediately call the NYPD. Isn't that indecent exposure? Just without the raincoat? And how the hell is that romantic? God help the boy who sends one of those to my daughters. I will cut that thing off.

I just don't understand the desire to be watched. For the sake of anthropological study, let me imagine how that experience—full exposure to the world, relayed with one click to Twitter—would unfold for me personally. Actually I'll take it a step further—I'll go all the way and imagine a sex tape. Merry Christmas, Mom!

First, location, location, location. I don't want to shoot in a hotel room mainly because I find room service too tempting. When you're at home the idea of making something to eat is so laborious, but the idea of making one call and getting anything you want? I would never get off the phone or let go of the menu! Safer to shoot it at home: I mean, what if school calls and one of the kids is sick? And I have Amazon packages coming. Plus, I know there are no bedbugs in my room. And as long as the dogs aren't sleeping on the comforter, it's quiet.

On to casting. My husband will say no to making a sex tape. Plus, I'm not sure I want him to get the audience's view of what I'm like in bed. There's a reason we have dimmer lights. And I can't offer the role to another man (or woman) because that's cheating. Even though I've always assured my husband it's just two actors playing roles . . . Anyway, it's just me. A one-woman show. Nobody else to steal the focus. By the way, I never understood in the Porn Academy awards what differentiates the categories between best actress and best supporting actress. Do you get relegated to supporting actress if you only cup the balls?

First problem: Where do I set up the camera or phone? I can prop my iPhone against a vase, but the second I go out of frame (not that I move all that much), there's no image. I could place it between my liquid melatonin and my antiaging, hydrating cream. But that's on the same level as the mattress and I've always heard you want the phone up high, aiming down. So I could duct-tape it to the ceiling, but how will I reach it to push play? So then I'm hiring a crew person, which costs money (and he would have to be union because I'm a member of SAG/AFTRA). The bigger issue is that I'm not on board with an audience. And what if the crew person is not attentive and plays Candy Crush the whole time? And forget a virtual audience—that would include relatives and old teachers.

And lighting! Do I go with natural daylight, which will only accentuate my cellulite and folds? Wait, I have neighbors. My bedroom opens up to a large Manhattan building and this show ain't free. (Plus, I'm pretty sure my dentist lives there.) I could rent some film lights from a production company. I'm sure the tattooed grip who's holding the phone could also adjust lighting. Except he's probably dismissive and judge-y. One thing that will help the lighting is body makeup. A bronze glittery lotion will even out skin tone and cover my chicken pox scars. But I can't ask the grip to also apply the body makeup in areas I can't reach.

So now I have to hire a makeup artist and we are talking serious coin! I could ask the woman who tints eyelashes at the local nail salon, but then I could never go back there, and it's just around the corner. And where will I go with an ingrown toenail?

Next, I'll need a protein shake. Or some kind of hydrating fruit-infused water. I don't have that, so I'll have ginger ale and a piece of cinnamon toast with extra butter. It's important to have something in your stomach before any strenuous activity. Preferably bland. And some omega-3 fish oil pills.

Shower time. I always forget to buy exfoliating scrub, but I do have kosher salt and some maple syrup and if I mix them together it should do the trick. Damn, all I have is some old homeopathic lice shampoo. So Ivory soap and a good conditioner will have to suffice. Of course, I need to shave my legs and armpits. It has been a while. Then I need to decide, what's sexier—wet hair? a slight wave? or hair up in a scrunchie? I think off the face. Crew guy (let's call him Dirk) agrees. He's vaping and checking the batteries in the boom.

What to wear, what to wear. You need a slow build. I don't own sexy lingerie. There are a few items hidden in the back of my sock drawer from my bridal shower, but leather makes me itch. And I can never figure out how to get out of a teddy—too many strings. I'll wear my beige fleece onesie with the hood. Yes, it makes me look like a fat bunny, but it's cozy. And it has a zipper down the front! (Sexy, sexy.)

As I brush my teeth, Dirk tells me all about his life in Williamsburg, Brooklyn, and his pansexuality. He has huge holes in his earlobes that hold what look like large round black camera batteries. Yes, tattoos everywhere, head shaved, save for a high man bun. He looks nonplussed by the project and somewhat repelled by me and my onesie. I don't want him to work hungry, so I make him a grilled cheese with heirloom tomatoes and a lemon soda. And give him a roll of frozen chocolate chip cookie dough to take home later.

I explain to Dirk that there's no plot. No pizza delivery-man. Just me. A monologue, kinda. Dirk excuses himself and uses my bathroom. Later it will take three hours, a plunger, and a can of Lysol spray to bring it back to its natural state. Plus, my retinol cream goes missing.

Dirk sets up two clip-on lights. And a mini tripod that holds my cell phone and my daughter's GoPro as a backup and for editing purposes. I ask Dirk if he can edit. "Yeah, I guess." I get a text from the makeup woman, Theresa, who says she's having bunion surgery and can't make it.

I've never seen Kim Kardashian's or any other of the many other blockbuster celebrity sex tapes, so I don't know if they used music or not. And if they did, it was probably their own? But since I've never "dropped a single," I put on Rachmaninoff's Piano Concerto No. 3. I find it sensual and provocative. Dirk puts in earbuds. He's listening to a band called Skin the Cat. And we're ready to shoot.

At this point, I'm exhausted. I have spent most of the day in preparation, and as is the case with every kid's birthday party I've produced, I am knackered. I need to take five, so I curl up on a pillow for a quick rest. I close my eyes.

When I wake up three hours later, Dirk is gone. I can hear the dogs barking in the kitchen and the kids giggling (I know immediately that they're eating frosting out of the can). I stretch and contemplate what kind of chicken to prepare for dinner. We had chicken the night before, but I hate to waste food and with enough sriracha and soy sauce they won't notice.

I keep the onesie on. Why not? I can just throw an apron over it and still be ready for bed later on!

As I leave my bedroom, I notice an invoice for $200 from Dirk and a note saying that he emailed me the video.

In it I'm napping with a tiny string of drool cascading down the right side of my mouth. It's not a traditional sex tape, but human sexuality is a curious thing and what is not sexy to one person may be to another. I grab my laptop and lock myself in the bathroom. The video goes on for about twenty minutes. In it, I'm still sleeping. At one point I snort. I send it to my agent to arrange the drop before it goes viral. And take a deep breath. I'm certain that I feel just like Kim Kardashian did just before her career sky-rocketed.

So if you're contemplating a little private tape just for your own personal viewing, always remember, it will get out. And everyone you know or don't know will see it. Yes, including your mother-in-law. And honestly, you never look as good naked as you think you do.

CHAPTER 20

CURSED

I think anyone who has children thinks they're parenting all wrong ALL the time. If you only feel it *sometimes* means you're doing something right. Or you're starting that bottle of wine too early in the day.

In all seriousness, I truly believe there is no right or wrong way to rear those little humans. Well, within the realm of acceptable and noncriminal behavior, and not in the stories you read in the *New York Post*. Anyway, when they grow up and write their own books about their scandalous childhoods, then you'll finally learn what you did wrong. The incomparable Joan Rivers delivered one of my all-time favorite parenting jokes: "All I heard when I was growing up was why can't you be like your cousin Sheila?

Why can't you be more like your cousin Sheila? . . . Sheila was stillborn."

Sometimes I think my husband and I are too lenient, compliant, and coddling. And sure, we are overcompensating for our own childhoods. But maybe our children could stand for us to be a little more callous. We've debated leaving them in Yosemite National Park with a Swiss Army knife and a can of tuna fish and allowing their survival instincts to kick in as they claw their way back to New York City. But I fear it's too late. They have an Uber app and can live for days on Reese's Pieces.

Chris Rock advocates bullying. He says if he hadn't been bullied as a child, he wouldn't be the man he is today. A successful comedian. But I'm not going to bully my daughters in the hopes that one day they can sell out the Barclays Center—I'm not so sure about their comedic timing. Still, I get the theory. Winston Churchill said, "Criticism may not be agreeable, but it is necessary. It fulfills the same function as pain in the human body. It calls attention to an unhealthy state of things." An astute observation, but before taking this as parenting advice, remember that his son Randolph was manic depressive, a womanizer, and a binge drinker.

We also don't believe in physical punishment. Belts are for keeping your pants up, brushes for detangling hair, and stun guns for waking up grandparents. But maybe we're wrong? Shock collars work on rambunctious Labrador retrievers, after all. (But then again there seems to be no pain as agonizing as when my girls have their phones taken away.) So we will just keep forcing them to sit with us and express their feelings—that seems like torture enough.

In superficial ways, I usually feel like a good mother. I make cupcakes that look like goblins on Halloween, bake banana bread for field hockey games, and decorate the Christmas tree every year (usually by myself). I leave love notes in duffels sent to sleepovers, camps, and school trips. I never say no to candy (mostly because I always want some, too). And I encourage my teenage girls to sleep with me when they feel stressed. It reminds me of the days when they were toddlers and had nightmares. Except they're much bigger now and kick harder.

I like to think they can discuss anything with me. As did my husband until the subject of vaginal discharge came up at dinner. I realized he has a limit.

Do I embarrass my children? Jesus, I hope so! That's my way of toughening them up. And if they rebel and make it their goal to become the opposite of me someday, then good on them, they will be dignified, elegant women. But until then . . . I will only wear pasties on late-night talk shows if there is a feminist statement behind it and refuse to believe it's *that* mortifying when I chase them around bar mitzvahs trying to get them to acknowledge my exemplary disco dancing.

I do use humor as a way to parent. I find it dissipates

any tense situations. My younger daughter had sex ed this year. She's my shy one. You know, she showers in a bathing suit. She was trying to assimilate all the words, ideas, and images that were discussed in the coed classroom that day. One being a poster of a penis that charted its progress in three stages: placid, semi-erect, and erect. I had to assure her that the penis did not have three rods sticking out of it. Men would be intolerable if that were true. (I mean, imagine teenage boys with three penises to deal with?) She told us that they had been discussing menstruation in another class and Eddy, the boy sitting next to her, started projectile vomiting and they had to stop class. Oh boy, Eddy . . . just you wait!

Then the following week, as we swirled our forks into turkey bolognese, our little girl put down her utensil, looked at us, and inquired, "Have you guys ever had anal sex?" And before my husband could clear his throat, I whispered to her, "Only for jewelry, sweetie."

If you're even thinking I am a terrible parent for falling back on humor to avoid a "teachable moment," I ask you: What are the alternatives? And by the way, why does a sixth grader even need to know such a thing? For her, the morning-after pill is a gummy omega-3 in the shape of a fish.

But all in all, I think I'm a decent parent. I walk them to the bus stop, go to all the holiday concerts, and never give them Benadryl just because we're on a long flight. But I did have an epic fail the other day. And my daughter will hold it against me for the rest of my life. Or her life, as she will live much longer . . .

———

Teenage girls tend to get fixated on a few things—YouTube videos, Netflix, models, Glossier makeup, and their period. When is it coming? What will it feel like? And will I suddenly feel like an adult? My older daughter hounded our pediatrician about it for over a year. "Can't you tell by my bones? Or pubic line? Or hand size?" She found it unbearably frustrating that it was not an exact science. If only she could know she was getting her period on November 4 at 5:30, she would be able to push her friend chat up to 6:30!

All through eighth grade, she would rush home to tell me who had gotten their period at school that day and who was still on the waitlist. This was a big deal.

Now, periods were never a discussion topic in my home when I was growing up. Because that all had to do with the business of vaginas and, God forbid, sex. I didn't want it, anticipate it, or pine for it. But for my daughter, it was the equivalent of getting pulled up onstage by Ed Sheeran.

At the same time that my daughter was awaiting the crimson tide, I was dealing with the opposite extreme: the onslaught of perimenopause. Something you most definitely do not look forward to. My daughter was anticipating the beginning of womanhood, I the demise. She the onset of fertility, me the atrophied tail end.

In my experience, one of the most unsettling side effects of perimenopause is the insomnia. I haven't experienced hot flashes or mood swings (aside from my usual chemical imbalances) or a deadened libido. Just abhorrent insomnia. Nights of tossing and turning. Sometimes nights of just getting up at three in the morning and having a bowl of cereal and catching up on old *Will & Grace* episodes. And there's no clearly identifiable source of stress driving this; my brain just won't shut down. And after two or three of these nights, I feel jet-lagged and nauseous. Any longer than that, I'm flat-out loopy.

It got so bad that I asked my internist what to do. I had tried the homeopathic road—herbs, primrose oil, sound machines, and crystals on my forehead. Nothing. So I figured it was time for some good old pharmaceutically backed Western medicine. The solution came in the form of a yellowish oval pill called Xanax. (These were mommy's candy—dolls, ladders, planks, tooties, xanies, Z-bars.) I was told by a certified physician to take a tiny crumb of one when exhibiting signs of unrest. Finally, a solution from the benzodiazepine family! Of course I never finished reading the list of potential side effects (they had me at depression and suicidal thoughts), but one possibility struck me as unusual—risk-taking behavior, that didn't sound so bad to me.

It was a fall evening. There was the usual homework panic, stacked dishes, and unruly dogs. I wore my most comfortable pajamas (from Target because they make the best, hands down) and had just finished reading a soothing section from *The Alchemist*. Our bedroom was lit with pink lightbulbs for a relaxing ambience. I spooned my husband and tried to will an eight-hour, level-four, deep sleep. Instead I boxed with my pillow and convinced myself I had a mosquito bite on my ankle. I kicked the covers off, then pulled them back up.

My husband's job requires him to wake up at 3:00 A.M. and consequently he is always out cold by 10:00 P.M. Not going through perimenopause himself, he sleeps like he's dead! I could have a teenage rave in our bedroom and he wouldn't stir. I popped out of bed and made my way to the bathroom for my new prescription. It took about twenty minutes before I could feel my muscles twitch and my brain get soft. And then I was OUT. Like Sunny von Bülow out. From that moment (when I was on the brink of flatlining) on, I remember nothing.

What follows is as told to me by my husband and daughter:

At midnight that night my older daughter ran into our bedroom, turned on the lights, and dove onto our bed. "I got my period," she shouted. Silence ensued. "MOM! Mommy! I just got my period!" My husband turned on his light.

"What did you get?" he asked. She gave him her usual eye roll and started tapping my shoulder.

"Mommmmmmm!!!!" I lay there like a fallen tree after a rainstorm. My husband checked my pulse. He quickly realized that he was literally the only parent there that night. And off he went with my new woman of a daughter to discuss all the wonderful ramifications of her discovery. I believe there were some awkward hugs and a few whispered congratulations. I mean no disrespect; what man in his fifties has the handbook on how to celebrate this milestone? But he did the best he could without having to pull up diagrams or PowerPoint boards or having the benefit of a torn paperback Judy Blume book.

The next morning I woke up like a newly born kitten. I rubbed my eyes, stretched, and licked my fur . . . or not that, but reached for my phone to check the time. What a wonderful, drug-induced night's sleep. I was more relaxed than I had been in decades. Until I found out what had transpired the night before.

My daughter was upset, to say the least. In fact, I'm not sure there is a word—not even an SAT word—that captures the full intensity of her rage and indignation. And for my part, I felt like the unluckiest woman alive. The one time, THE ONE TIME, I was not available . . . What are the odds that the one time I decide to pill pop, this happens?

Needless to say, my daughter can hold a grudge. When she was four years old, we were on vacation and she begged my husband and me to take her with us to a New Year's Eve party at the resort. We placated her by saying we would, then put her to bed at the usual bedtime. Again, she was four years old. When we got home at 1:00 A.M. she was sitting on her bed in a party dress, Mary Janes, and a sparkling headband. The hotel babysitter (who we suspected was stoned) was passed out in a chair. I've never heard my daughter cry so loudly. My husband had to carry her off the hotel property so as to avoid getting kicked out. And she brings this up at least forty times a year. The night her parents first disappointed her.

Now here was another. I had failed my daughter during a landmark event. Not on purpose! The pills made me do it. But I was so crestfallen. She marched into the kitchen in her striped blue uniform skirt and white sweatshirt. A new woman. A new, angry woman. And disappeared into the October day. October 12, 2017.

I was riddled with guilt. Not only because I hadn't been there for a very critical moment in her life, but also because I realized I loved Xanax. I felt like the husband who forgot the anniversary; no way were flowers the day after going to cut it. But I had to try. When she returned home that afternoon, I had placed a huge menstruation gift basket on her bed—panty liners, a heating pad, chocolate bars, Motrin, more chocolate, a PMS stress ball, frozen cookie dough, and maxipads.

She smirked. I took it as a smirk of forgiveness. I perched next to her on the bed (still strewn with stuffed animals) and took a deep breath. "I'm so sorry I was asleep last night. I just hadn't slept in days and I really needed a good night's sleep."

She unwrapped a Twix bar. "That's okay."

"And I'm sorry I wasn't there for you at such an important moment. You know I want to be part of all the milestones in your life. Will you forgive me?"

There was a long pause.

"I forgive you. Plus, I don't think it was my period. . . ."

"I'm sorry, what do you mean you don't think it was your period?"

"Well, there was no actual blood."

"No blood at all?"

"Nope." She continued to eat her Twix bar.

"So . . . why did you say you got your period?"

"I don't know . . . it was just a feeling . . ."

"A feeling?"

"All right, God! I guess I was wrong!"

And that, folks, is the ride I call motherhood! Are you there God? It's me, Ali.

CHAPTER 21

TWENTY THINGS I KNOW FOR SURE

1. Always celebrate your birthday. Even when you're in your eighties. In life, there are so few excuses to consume a Carvel ice cream cake.

2. Get the shingles vaccine. Or lie in bed for three weeks with a herpes rash across your face. Kills your sex life.

3. Invest in a good dermatologist. Let's be honest, the face is what everyone sees. And I don't know what a butt-enhancing doctor is called.

4. If you have the sense that someone is following you, someone probably is.

5. If someone ever asks, "If you could go back in time and kill Hitler, would you?" The answer is always YES!

6. If you drop your cell phone in a public toilet—LEAVE IT!

7. When they're teenagers, get your kids a photo book of sexually transmitted diseases. Show it to their friends.

8. Always tip at least 20 percent. Or enjoy a toenail in your salad the next time.

9. Force yourself to read the news. Your eyes may glaze over deciphering fiscal responsibility, but the gossip column can be your treat after you're done.

10. Don't stalk anyone, lest you be stalked yourself.

11. Take 2 tablespoons of apple cider vinegar every morning. Natural diuretic. Plus I just want to see if you'll do it.

12. Just say No. Loudly. And carry a whistle.

13. Wear sunscreen. Nobody told me to and I have the damage to show for it.

14. Don't put cashmere in the dryer. You'll see.

15. Do something charitable; get involved in community service. Even narcissists need a break from themselves. Selflessness is what separates us humans from the animals.

16. Don't pet a snake. Even if she seems nice.

17. If you meet someone and they seem crazy—they are!

18. At least once in your life try ham and pineapple pizza.

19. No matter what anyone says, navy and black do go together.

20. Don't dye your hair pink or blue if you're over sixteen years old.

hope that I have in some way enlightened you. Maybe even about checking your email before hitting send? I mean, I know you're going to make a sex tape anyway. . . .

I am an entertainer, but if you pay me I can also be your guru or life coach. Well, it doesn't have to be money, I do many arduous things for snacks! But for years people have asked me for my advice and while for the first forty years I was dry as a bone, I know I am pretty confident about pulling polished philosophical gems out of my ass.

My main point—and the reason you should buy this book for all your family and friends—is, sharing wisdom is everything. We can learn by one another's trials and errors. Sure, maybe you've made more mistakes than me, but ultimately, these mishaps will enrich your life and the tales will be fruitful for others. And this book, full of my stories, can perhaps save you the time of experiencing the same painful, pie-in-your-face events that have made me who I am. My own failures and pitfalls. Oh, and rewards too!

We all have our stories. Even Gandhi did some dumbass things as a teenager.

And to conclude I leave you with one more crumb:

DYING'S NOT SO BAD. YOU'LL FINALLY HAVE AN EXCUSE NOT TO ANSWER ALL THOSE TEXTS.

—ALI WENTWORTH

ACKNOWLEDGMENTS

My book is nothing without my editor, Jennifer Barth. In fact my book without her, is not a book. It's some scribblings on a Post-it. Jennifer even scheduled a photo session for the cover before I formulated what the book was about. THAT's a damn good editor.

I have to thank everyone at HarperCollins for believing in me, pushing me, and squeezing blood from a stone.

My book agent, Jennifer Joel, at ICM who's much smarter than me, but don't tell her. For Ted Chervin, Courtney Catzel, Kaitlyn Flynn, Ruthann Secunda, Steven Brown, Pete Stone, and the whole team at ICM that support me even though I'm in the lower earnings bracket. Is it my baked goods?

My lawyer, Adam Kaller—who has not had to post bail yet.

For all my girlfriends, who hold my hand, make me laugh, and offer the best advice.

ACKNOWLEDGMENTS

My parents and siblings, who give me plenty of material and who I'm pleased to say I have a thriving, close, and loving relationship with.

To my husband, who is better than me, but doesn't push my face in it and allows me to make mistakes without penalties. And allows me to be the clown.

And to my two beautiful daughters—I could write a book every single day about how amazing you each are. That would make HarperCollins very happy. . . .

ABOUT THE AUTHOR

ALI WENTWORTH is the author of *Ali in Wonderland* and *Happily Ali After*. The star of the comedy series *Nightcap*, she made a name for herself on the sketch comedy show *In Living Color*, and her film credits include *Jerry Maguire*, *The Real Blonde*, *Office Space*, and *It's Complicated*. A native of Washington, D.C., she lives in New York City with her husband, George Stephanopoulos, and their two daughters.